Raising the
Shy Child

A Parent's Guide to Social Anxiety
Raising the Shy Child

Advice for Helping Kids Make Friends, Speak Up, and Stop Worrying

Christine Fonseca

PRUFROCK PRESS INC.
WACO, TEXAS

Dedication

This book is for everyone who felt too shy and too scared to face the day. I promise brighter times are possible.

Library of Congress Cataloging-in-Publication Data

Fonseca, Christine, 1966-
  Raising the shy child : a parent's guide to social anxiety / by Christine Fonseca.
      pages cm
  Includes bibliographical references.
  ISBN 978-1-61821-398-3 (pbk.)
  1. Bashfulness in children. 2. Social phobia in children. 3. Child rearing. 4. Parenting. I. Title.
  BF723.B3F66 2015
  649'.15--dc23
                              2014048544

Edited by Lacy Compton

Layout design by Raquel Trevino

ISBN-13: 978-1-61821-398-3

At the time of this book's publication, all facts and figures cited are the most current available; all telephone numbers, addresses, and website URLs are accurate and active; all publications, organizations, websites, and other resources exist as described in this book; and all have been verified. The authors and Prufrock Press make no warranty or guarantee concerning the information and materials given out by organizations or content found at websites, and we are not responsible for any changes that occur after this book's publication. If you find an error or believe that a resource listed here is not as described, please contact Prufrock Press.

Prufrock Press Inc.
P.O. Box 8813
Waco, TX 76714-8813
Phone: (800) 998-2208
Fax: (800) 240-0333
http://www.prufrock.com

Table of Contents

Acknowledgements...ix

Author's Note...xi

Introduction...xiii

Part I. When Shyness Becomes a Problem

Chapter 1. Understanding Social Anxiety 3

Chapter 2. The Biology of Anxiety...27

Chapter 3. Environmental Causes of Social Anxiety 43

Chapter 4. The Impact of Social Anxiety..................................69

Part II. Feeling Safe Inside Your Skin

Chapter 5. Social Anxiety Comes to School.............................93

Chapter 6. Social Anxiety and Friendships............................109

Chapter 7. Social Anxiety in the World..................................123

Part III. Creating Safe Havens

Chapter 8. How to Help..137

Chapter 9. Developing an Action Plan for Home 151

Chapter 10. When to Seek Additional Help 167

Part IV. Social Anxiety FAQs

Chapter 11. Social Anxiety 101 185

Chapter 12. Social Skills and More: Specific Questions
Regarding SAD 193

Chapter 13. Educators Ask Questions....................................201

Final Thoughts 211

References 213

About the Author..223

Acknowledgements

Writing is never a solitary sport. And bringing to life a book like this always takes the help of many in order to make it relevant. This list I'm certain is not exhaustive, but it does represent those without whom this book would not exist.

To Lacy Compton and the team at Prufrock Press—once again your support, encouragement, and insistence on quality continues to grow my art and provide a platform from which I can help others. "Thank you" hardly seems adequate!

To my writing partner, Michelle McLean—once again I must thank you for dropping what you're doing and taking a few moments to read and provide suggestions on another one of my books. One day I'll figure out how to repay you for this!

To my real-life BFFs and cheer squad: Jodi, Kelley, Nancy, Jill, Corrine, Joe, Debbi, and Andrea—You are all such amazing friends and supporters of what I strive to do on a daily basis. Thank you for being willing to share stories, lend an ear, and just help when I need it. Trust me when I say that it never goes unnoticed.

To Nancy Lewis and Jodi Curtis—Thank you for the last minute information on all things speech and language related and for pointing me in the right direction for some resources. I am so fortunate to be surrounded by such talent every day.

To the hundreds of contributors from more than five countries— Your stories filled these pages and made my words more relevant than they would have been otherwise. Thank you for allowing me to be part of your lives and sharing your struggles and triumphs, your opinions, and questions. Although there were too many of you to name specifically, I do want to send a special shout-out to Erin, Gina, Sarah, Brittany, and the others who wished to remain anonymous in the book. You guys are fearless. Thank you!

To the endless sea of support from the writing community, the bloggers, readers, and fangirls I never dreamed I'd have—I haven't met most of you in real life, but wowza! You guys are really amazing. Your encouragement and understanding of the industry we all love is nothing short of amazing.

Finally, my acknowledgements are never complete without a personal thank you to my family, both immediate and extended.

To Dirck, Fabiana, and Erika—You are my life. Period. None of this would happen without your support and willingness to share me with my stories and my readers.

To my extended family—Thanks for making sure my hubby and kids don't feel too neglected when I'm under deadline. Thank you, also, for reminding me that there is a life beyond my books! The balance means everything. And no, I'm really not as stressed as I may seem from time to time!

—Christine Fonseca

Author's Note

As a practicing school psychologist, I have been on the frontline of the mental health crisis facing many school-aged children for almost two decades. These children increasingly suffer from mental health concerns inadequately addressed in private or public sectors, often resulting in significant impacts to educational functioning.

Perhaps the most common mental health concerns I deal with in my daily job are anxiety and social phobia. Ranging from the mild case of performance anxiety to the more significant bouts of school refusal, agoraphobia, and selective mutism, children from kindergarten through high school are stretched to their limits. They're asked to demonstrate coping skills beyond their capacity in order to deal with our ever-increasing stressful world, often with disastrous results that include increased school refusal, behavioral problems, suicidal ideations, and reduced resiliency.

Most of my work with parents, educators, and children has focused on developing strategies for daily use to negate the negative impact caused by everyday stress. Through this work, I've witnessed the lack of information for parents regarding the causes and treatment of anxiety in general, and social anxiety more specifically. Without this information, parents are left to feel hopeless in the face of their children's resistance toward building friendships, lack of self-advocacy, and school refusal.

It is my goal that this book will provide some of the much needed answers in this area. Based on both my professional experience and the most recent, though limited, research on social anxiety in children and adolescents, this book strives to put into user-friendly language the science behind social anxiety. In addition, I've collected the best evidence-based interventions and tips to provide parents and children with the tools needed to end their cycle of embarrassment and humiliation and develop the skills needed in our complex social world.

Finally, it is my desire that anyone dealing with social anxiety knows that he or she is not alone in this struggle. As one of my contributors to this project said, "Before I knew I had the disorder, I (had) never met anyone with it, or knew it had a name." I've included case studies and direct quotes from the people impacted by social anxiety disorder throughout the book. Although I have changed the names and any identifying information to protect the participants' anonymity, it is my hope that these real-world stories will remind readers confronted with the issues presented in this book that they are not alone.

I want to extend a quick thanks to those individuals brave enough to share their thoughts, their stories, and their time with me. Social anxiety is a challenging beast. My hope is that with increased knowledge and understanding, we can find a way past the fear together.

—Christine Fonseca

Introduction

Clutching her hands, nervously biting his lips, repeatedly checking her phone—take a look around any school hallway during passing periods, and chances are you'll find a few students demonstrating these or similar signs of building anxiety. Look harder, and you may find a few that are rocking back and forth, hiding, or silently crying in the bathroom, indications of more significant levels of anxiety and fear. An estimated 9%–12% of the population (children, adolescents, and adults) is affected by social anxiety either by itself or alongside other mental health concerns (Ruscio et al., 2008; Wittchen, Stein, & Kessler, 1999). Furthermore, social anxiety disorder has been identified as one of the most common mental health concerns in children and adolescents after depression and substance abuse (Bernstein, 2014; Kashdan & Herbert, 2001). Despite its prevalence, social anxiety is one of the least researched, diagnosed, and treated mental health conditions (Kashdan & Herbert, 2001), especially in children and adolescents.

The impact of social anxiety disorder (SAD), formerly called social phobia (American Psychiatric Association, 2013b), can be quite significant in children and adolescents. Ranging from reduced social competence to social pessimism and poor resiliency development (Kashdan & Herbert, 2001), it is not surprising that schools and parents continue to seek out ways to counteract the negative impact of social anxiety problems and get help for their children.

Unfortunately, finding help is more than a little challenging. Previously viewed as a matter of temperament and not having a significant negative impact to children, social anxiety has only recently elevated to an area of concern (Beidel & Turner, 2007). I can tell you from personal experience in my work as a school psychologist that the impact of SAD on children, parents, and educators is extreme. Faced with children whose behavior ranges from severe crying jags to complete withdrawal from social situations, parents are increasingly forced to navigate through the maze of mental health to find ways to help their children, often with mixed results.

Enter *Raising the Shy Child: A Parent's Guide to Social Anxiety*. Designed to provide a bridge between research, clinical practice, and daily application, *Raising the Shy Child* combines research, best practice, case studies, and personal anecdotes in a user-friendly style for parents and educators alike. *Raising the Shy Child* addresses:

- the current definition of social anxiety disorder, including the science of social anxiety, environmental factors, and treatment options;
- the similarities and differences between introversion, shyness, and social anxiety disorder;
- the impact of giftedness, speech and language or learning concerns, and autism spectrum disorder on social anxiety;
- working with social anxiety at school, at home, and with friends;
- specific strategies addressing bullying, resiliency, perfectionism, and school refusal; and
- the influence of cultural factors and issues surrounding sexual identity on social anxiety disorder.

How to Use This Book

Raising the Shy Child is specifically designed to be a user-friendly resource for parents and educators. Section I establishes a foundation of understanding, with chapters that discuss the science of social anxiety and its impact on daily functioning. Section II addresses the particular problems social anxiety disorder may manifest within the school, social (peer), and home settings, as well as practical interventions designed to improve outcomes. Section III focuses on treatment options for private and educational use. The final section offers a "frequently asked questions" (FAQ) section to investigate specific questions in all areas of SAD.

The chapters within each section are set up to include anecdotal stories from parents and children who are dealing with social anxiety disorder, as well as case studies highlighting the real-world examples of social anxiety. In addition, each chapter addresses specific situations related to the complexities of social anxiety, tips and strategies for parents and children, and a section for educators. You'll find many questionnaires, worksheets, and tip sheets to help you and your child on the journey to overcoming social anxiety. You can find reproducible copies of these forms at http://www.prufrock.com/Assets/ClientPages/Shy_Child.aspx

A Word to Educators

Raising the Shy Child is written specifically for parents, but that does not mean I ignored the needs of teachers, school counselors and psychologists, and school administrators. The "Chalk Talk" section within each chapter addresses specific aspects of social anxiety disorder as it relates to the classroom environment. Covering topics that range from understanding SAD in the classroom to creating a culture of caring, *Raising the Shy Child* is an excellent resource for teachers as well as parents. It is my hope that the suggestions offered within these pages will result in a stronger collaboration between parents and educators and improved outcomes for students wrestling with social anxiety disorder. Other topics of discussion in *Raising the Shy Child* include:

- introversion and SAD—understanding the differences and similarities in the classroom;
- embedding coping skills and social skills into the curriculum;
- what to do when bully prevention programs fail;
- supporting students and parents struggling with school refusal; and
- creating reasonable action plans for students that yield positive results.

Educators are an important part of the support network children with SAD need in order to work past their fears and begin living without their often crippling anxiety.

A Word to Children and Teens

Raising the Shy Child may talk to the important adults in your lives, but it was written for you as well. Every story, question, intervention, and topic came from my direct experiences in working with children of all ages dealing with various degrees of social anxiety. In nearly two decades of work, I have learned many things about children and anxiety—the most important of which is that living with anxiety does not have to be a crippling experience. You can overcome the fears and learn to recognize them for what they are—a call to attention that something is bothering you, causing a measure of discomfort. Anxiety in and of itself is not a bad thing. It is just part of what it means to be human. The trick is learning to discern when you need to act and what action to take.

As your parents work through the book and find ways to support you, I encourage you to look through the book as well. Read the worksheets and the tips, read the case studies and quotes, and discover your own unique path to overcoming the negative aspects of social anxiety.

PART I

When Shyness Becomes a Problem

CHAPTER 1

Understanding Social Anxiety

"The biggest challenge we face with social anxiety is the energy it takes from me when I have to participate in social situations that are overwhelming. I become exhausted and edgy. My daughter also suffers from this, and it is difficult to watch as a parent. I have a hard time with strategies for her because I understand what she is going through and want to protect her from the feelings." —Erin, parent and adult with social anxiety

Nine-year-old Jaymie loves to hang out with her sister, playing dress-up and pretending that she is on Broadway. She could spend all day staring in the mirror, lip-syncing her favorite songs and dancing. In an effort to support Jaymie's Broadway dreams, her mom enrolled her in a theatre-dance class and the local children's theatrical group. Jaymie was thrilled—until the first day came.

Instead of excitement, Jaymie was struck with fear. Her hands began to sweat, and her heart pounded in her chest. She bit her nails and mumbled to her mom that she didn't want to go to the class after all. In fact, maybe she didn't want to be on Broadway. In her mind, she was already justifying her actions, and telling herself that her lack of talent would result in disaster. She imagined the humiliation she'd face from her peers.

At first glance, it would be easy to think that Jaymie was just overly shy. An introvert by nature, Jaymie did tend to avoid new social situations. She has demonstrated shyness from time to time, but not to this extent, and certainly never enough to keep her from doing something she loves.

At least, not until now.

So what happened? What prevented Jaymie from being able to participate in something she had dreamed about doing? Her temperament? Shyness? Perhaps. However, Jaymie's symptoms could also point to something more significant—social anxiety disorder, or SAD.

Before we get too far into a discussion of what SAD is or is not, I want you to take a moment and reflect on your own opinions of shyness, social anxiety and the impact of these on your children and family, using Worksheet #1.

Social Anxiety Disorder: A Definition

Social anxiety is nothing new in the mental health field. Previously identified as everything from social fear to social neurosis (Schilder, 1938) to social phobia (American Psychiatric Association, 2013a), social anxiety disorder is characterized by an intense fear of socializing with others that results in extreme self-consciousness, negative self-evaluations, and eventually, social avoidance (Richards, 2014).

As stated in the Introduction, SAD impacts roughly 9%–12% of the overall population (Ruscio et al., 2008; Wittchen et al., 1999). It is considered both one of the most common mental health concerns in children and adolescents (Bernstein, 2014; Kashdan & Herbert, 2001), as well as a condition with one of the earliest onsets (Beidel & Turner, 2007). Research indicates the typical age of diagnosis for general social anxiety disorder is between ages 7 and 13. Furthermore, adults with social anxiety reported feeling disruptive levels of fear and stress early in their childhood. In my own work within the school setting, parents with a history of social anxiety have reported that they began feeling anxious in early elementary school. The teens I work with also report feeling strong levels of anxiety throughout their early childhood experiences.

The definition of SAD has been broadened and clarified in the current revision of the *Diagnostic and Statistical Manual of Mental Disorders* (DSM-5; American Psychiatric Association, 2013a) to include the following characteristics:

Worksheet #1

Ideas About Shyness, Social Anxiety, and My Family

Directions: Take a moment to read and answer each question. Revisit these questions as your thoughts and opinions change.

1. What are your definitions of shyness, introversion, and social anxiety?
2. The biggest challenge I or my child faces with social anxiety is . . . *(complete the sentence)*
3. How does social anxiety impact you or your family?
4. What interventions for shyness or social anxiety have worked the best for you or your child?
5. Do your relatives deal with issues related to shyness or social anxiety? What are they?

Once you are finished, take a moment to reflect on your answers and consider the following questions: What are the reasons you picked up this book? What are you hoping to get out of it? In what ways are you hoping to help your children? Take a moment to write down your thoughts regarding shyness, social anxiety, and your goals for reading this book.

- unreasonable fear in social situations, disproportionate to the actual event;
- exposure to the feared situation causes significant levels of anxiety, distress, or avoidance;
- the anxiety, distress, or avoidance results in a significant disruption of daily life functioning;
- the fear, anxiety, or avoidance must have a duration of more than 6 months; and
- the fear, anxiety, or avoidance cannot be caused by a substance abuse or a secondary condition (i.e., stuttering) unless the reaction is significantly more than typical given the situation.

As you can tell by the definition, SAD is beyond shyness or social communication concerns (American Psychiatric Association, 2013b). It is a debilitating condition that can significantly impact normal functioning and social development, especially in children.

There are a couple of significant points to the criteria listed above. First, the duration period of 6 months is important. Social stress, even to the point of social anxiety, often occurs throughout a person's lifetime (Bogels et al., 2010). This is particularly true with children as they progress through the various development and social stages of life—the first day of school, the first time performing or speaking, being attracted to someone else for the first time. Each of these major events can trigger a series of intense responses. It is important to distinguish these events from SAD. A true case of social anxiety will significantly impact a person to the point of avoidance and extreme distress. This is not a just a case of needing time to warm-up to a social situation. It is so much more.

Another important consideration within the criteria is the idea of a disproportionate fear. Think about the last time you or your child was reticent to join a social situation. Perhaps the activity involved a person with whom you had a tumultuous relationship. Perhaps your child was bullied in the past and is, therefore, nervous about being in a similar situation. If this is the case, experiencing a measure of fear or anxiety, even if an intense one, is not unwarranted. In fact, I would argue that if the situation had been particularly traumatic, I would *expect* you to feel significant levels of stress at the mere thought of engaging with that person in any way again.

In this situation, the anxiety and fear are not indicators of SAD. Yes, they are difficult to endure. You will likely want to use some of the strategies incorporated within the book to assist with managing your or your child's response, but the fear is not an indication of social anxiety because your reaction, or the reaction of your child, is expected within the context. I will expand on this topic more as we get into conversations about gifted children and anxiety, as well as misdiagnosis and comorbid conditions in Chapter 4.

Early versions of the DSM-5 considered separating SAD into different subtypes, including a generalized subtype that encompassed people diagnosed with SAD in which the disorder occurred across multiple settings and situations, and specific subtypes based on the type and degree of fear experienced. A review of relevant research, however, does not support the majority of specifiers, including and most significantly, the generalized SAD subtype. Rather, SAD is best conceptualized as occurring on a continuum based on the number and intensity of fear-evoking or avoidant situations (Bogels et al., 2010; Stein, Torgrud, & Walker, 2000).

This is not to say that all people with SAD, regardless of severity, are the same. In fact, research suggests that people with a greater number of fear-evoking situations and a more severe reaction are typically diagnosed at a younger age, and are more significantly impacted throughout their lifespan. Furthermore, while they are equally responsive to treatment, people with a more generalized social anxiety have a greater likelihood for comorbidity with depression and substance abuse (Bogels et al., 2010; Mesa, Nieves, & Beidel, 2011; Stein et al., 2000). Despite the relatively arbitrary distinctions made based on amount and type of fear, most clinicians recommend the continued used of subtypes with reference to treatment goals and outcomes (Stein et al., 2000).

There is one SAD specifier supported by the research that is included in the DSM-5—social anxiety disorder, performance only type. Defined as people whose fear is limited to performance situations like public speaking or performing, this subtype often demonstrates a milder set of symptoms including less behavioral inhibition and a later age of onset (typically during mid-adolescence). Furthermore, people with this type of SAD typically report a stronger physiological response to their anxiety and fear, including headaches, heart palpitations, and a sense of panic. Even the cause of this type of SAD appears to be more related to traumatic events than to a familial or neurobiological link (Bogels et al., 2010).

All in all, social anxiety disorder exists across the lifetime. The heart of the disorder, persistent and intense fear of being negatively scrutinized by others, occurs in children, teens, and adults, although the specific presentation of the anxiety looks different based on the specific stage of development (Mesa et al., 2011). This book will focus on the presentation and treatment of SAD in children and teens, as well as proactive interventions to help prevent the initial development of SAD, if possible, and reduce the duration when it does occur.

Symptoms

Researchers typically view anxiety as a constellation of three distinct parts: physical symptoms, cognitive beliefs, and behavioral actions or avoidance (Lang, 1968). These aspects of social anxiety form the foundation of understanding the disorder, and more importantly, determining how to intervene and support the person experiencing SAD.

Before we get into the specific symptomology, take a moment to consider the following questionnaire. Go through each question and indicate your answers as they relate to your children and anyone else wrestling with social anxiety. Although this questionnaire in no way indicates whether or not you or a loved one meets criteria for a diagnosis of SAD, nor is it meant to replace appropriate diagnostic procedures, it can provide insight to you with regard to the specific way(s) social anxiety is currently manifesting in your child. After you've completed the questionnaire, have your child complete it also and compare both sets of responses. Then take a look at the more common symptoms related to social anxiety and their implications for treatment.

Questionnaire #1
Social Anxiety Symptoms Checklist

Directions: Read each statement and decide if you agree, disagree, or neither agree nor disagree with the statements as they relate to your child. Check the appropriate box for your answers. When you have completed the questionnaire, have your child complete a separate questionnaire. Add up the totals for each and compare the results.

	I agree	I disagree	I neither agree nor disagree
I am very afraid of making a mistake in front of other people.			
I am afraid I will do something embarrassing in front of others every day.			
I am always judged by others, and usually in a negative way.			
My fear of being embarrassed prevents me from speaking up in class.			
My fear of saying something embarrassing keeps me from going to parties or other social activities.			
When I have to give an oral presentation in class, I think and worry about the event for days or weeks before.			
I consider myself to be very awkward socially.			
When I have to go to a party with unfamiliar people, I often get headaches or stomachaches.			
Meeting new people is very hard for me.			
I avoid social situations because they are too hard for me.			
My fear of being embarrassed or humiliated by others keeps me from going to school.			
My fear of being embarrassed or humiliated by others keeps me from making new friends.			
My fear of behavior embarrassed or humiliated by others keeps me from going to social events.			

	I agree	I disagree	I neither agree nor disagree
People say I am negative about social situations.			
Most people say I am overly negative about my performance at school.			

Count up the "I agree" answers for both the questionnaire completed by you and the one completed by your child. The more "I agree" answers you have, the greater the impact shyness and/or social anxiety has in your child's life. Take a moment to reflect on the questionnaire, paying particular attention to the ways in which the two questionnaires are the same and how they are different. Write any new insights on the lines below.

_____

_____

_____

_____

_____

_____

_____

_____

_____

_____

_____

_____

_____

_____

_____

_____

_____

_____

_____

Physical Symptoms

The psychophysiological aspects of SAD are evident throughout the research. Physical manifestations of anxiety appear in children and teens with SAD in response to specific fear-evoking situations, in anticipation of the events, and in some cases, when remembering the event (Mesa et al., 2011). More typical symptoms reported by children and teens include:

- feeling light-headed,
- heart palpitations,
- feeling flushed or chilled,
- headaches,
- choking,
- nausea, and
- shaky hands.

Additionally, adolescents report feelings consistent with panic attacks, although this is somewhat uncommon (Beidel & Turner, 2007).

Many of us can relate to feeling some of these physical symptoms when we encounter anxiety. For a child or teen with SAD, however, the physical symptoms are unrelenting and all consuming. Many of the children I've worked with have described it as "feeling like the walls were closing in, and you're drowning." No wonder most children become avoidant when they encounter this level of anxiety.

Self-reporting is not the only way researchers and clinicians have become aware of the physical aspects of social anxiety. Early experiments utilizing blood pressure and heart rate measurements in adolescents during role-playing activities suggest the presence of an actual physiological change in response to anxiety (Beidel, Turner, & Dancu, 1985). Although more recent research suggests a reduced physiological response to social anxiety (Mesa et al., 2011), anecdotal stories from my own work, as well as accounts from clinicians, point to the activation of our natural fight-or-flight response when faced with anxiety as intense as that found in children diagnosed with SAD.

I will expand on the biological aspects of SAD more in Chapter 2. For now, I'd like you to think of the physical symptoms of social anxiety as the body's natural warning system. As with any warning system, there are early indicators that stress is increasing. Part of managing anxiety and reducing the impact of social anxiety involves understanding your child's specific early warning signs of distress and engaging in a specific intervention(s) prior to the activation of full-blown fight-or-flight response.

Take a moment to work through the following worksheet with your child. Go through each question together and help him or her answer the questions. Then have your child make his or her own Early Warning System chart. This activity will help both of you begin to understand all of the early signs that a major anxiety attack is coming, and hopefully prevent the full force of its impact.

Cognitive Beliefs

One of the cornerstone aspects of social anxiety is the paralyzing fear of humiliation and embarrassment by a child's peers. This fear can take the form of excessive worrying, significant negative thought patterns and negative evaluation, or avoidance (Beidel & Turner, 2007). Most commonly, the cognitive beliefs involve an often faulty perception of failure. Children and adolescents with SAD anticipate failure within the fear-inducing event more frequently and to a greater degree than their nonanxious peers (Cartwright-Hatton, Tschernitz, & Gomersall, 2005). They worry about appearing nervous and making mistakes during tasks, as well as how others will perceive their actions. Even when these children perform well, they tend to hyperfocus on their perceived mistakes instead of accurately recalling performance.

It is important to note that this is another area of some controversy within the research. Other experiments similar to the Cartwright-Hatton study indicated that adolescents with SAD did anticipate failure more readily than their nonanxious peers, but also performed weaker than students without anxiety (Alfano, Beidel, & Turner, 2006; Mesa et al., 2011). Whether this is a by-product of their avoidance of these types of stress-inducing activities or an indication that there is a lack of specific social competencies is still unclear.

What is certain is that socially anxious children and adolescents engage in a pattern of faulty thinking that often results in avoidant

Worksheet #2

My Early Warning Signs

Directions: For each step, write down physical and emotional symptoms as indicated. Complete the questions at the end and make a list of your specific stress cycle.

Steps	Physical Signs (How does your body feel? What areas are tense?)	Emotional Signs (How do you feel? What is your emotional state?)
Step 1: Watch an action movie or play an action-packed video game. Pay attention to your physical and emotional symptoms during the movie or game and write them down.		
Step 2: During your next quiz or test, notice your physical and emotional symptoms/behaviors and write them down.		
Step 3: The next time you go to a party or social event, notice your physical and emotional symptoms/behaviors and write them down.		

Look over your answers above. Do you notice any similarities? Differences? Take the similarities and indicate them on the lines below. Start with the first symptom, then the next until you've determined your stress cycle.

_____

_____

_____

_____

_____

_____

_____

behavior. This creates a never-ending cycle in which the child struggles with a task, feels a heightened level of anxiety and humiliation, avoids a similar task in the future, and weakens his or her original skills at the task because he or she is not getting practice. Before long, it is nearly impossible to determine if the socially anxious child's deficits involve faulty cognition or social skills deficits, and perhaps the distinction is no longer necessary. Regardless of how the problem started, the child now requires assistance with both his or her faulty thinking and social competency.

Behavioral Actions or Avoidance

Speaking of avoidant behavior, children and adolescents with SAD engage in many forms of behavior avoidance, ranging from classic social event avoidance to a more subtle covert behavior of avoiding eye contact or avoiding being in the spotlight (Mesa et al., 2011). Children will not often report these behaviors as avoidant. Their perceptions of their behaviors often skew toward the positive, something that changes as children develop into adolescents. This is part of the reason behind the DSM-5's change in the diagnostic procedure for children to be less reliant on self-reporting (American Psychiatric Association, 2013b).

As children mature, and social engagement becomes less parent driven and more independent, avoidant behaviors among adolescents with SAD increase, often resulting in impaired social relationships. The cycle begins again and socially anxious adolescents are faced with a never-ending pattern of avoidance, reduced friendships, increased loneliness, and more avoidance (Mesa et al., 2011).

One way to break the cycle of avoidance is to understand what types of situations lead to the behavior in the first place. Questionnaire #2 was developed to help children identify the kinds of social situations that cause anxiety, as well as quantify the level of anxiety the situation produces. Complete the worksheet independently for your child. Then have your child complete the exercise and compare the results. This will help you understand not only the types of situations that cause increased fear, but also the degree of anxiety. It will also help you discover how accurately your child views his or her specific behaviors, something vital to knowing which interventions to attempt.

Questionnaire #2

How Avoidant Is My Child?

Directions: Read each statement and decide if it is true for you all of the time, some of the time, or none of the time. Check the appropriate box. Add up totals for each answer at the end.

	All	Some	None
I avoid situations in which I have to meet new people.			
I avoid thinking about social events.			
I avoid going to parties or other social events.			
I prefer to work alone instead of in a group.			
I avoid speaking out in class.			
I avoid asking the teacher questions unless no one else is around.			
I avoid thinking about tests or oral presentations.			
I don't like asking others for help.			
I avoid asking for directions.			
If I try to speak up in class, my stress will increase.			
If I try to attend a party or other social event, I will feel very anxious.			
If I try to meet new friends, I will fail at it.			
If I try to ask for help, other people will laugh at me.			
I worry when I take a test.			
I worry when my family is not with me.			

Total your responses. List the "all" statements on the lines below. These are the areas that cause the most internal stress and should be addressed. Repeat this exercise periodically throughout the year.

_____

_____

_____

_____

_____

_____

_____

_____

Avoidant behaviors are not the only way in which social anxiety manifests in children and adolescents. Nervous behaviors, including picking, nail biting, a shaky voice, and mumbling are also indicators of anxiety (Beidel & Turner, 2007). The presence of these behaviors during specific social activities, as well as a reprise of the behavior when the child is anticipating or recalling the events is a good indication that the child may be dealing with a case of social anxiety. It is important to understand these symptoms in order to choose which proactive intervention can best assist the child.

What Social Anxiety Is Not

As important as it is to understand what social anxiety is and how those symptoms are manifesting in your child, it is equally important to understand what social anxiety is not. As I stated earlier, SAD is not a matter of shyness, introversion, or overexciteabilities run amok. It is a distinct anxiety disorder with its own etiology as indicated throughout the chapter. It does mirror several other disorders, and it can be comorbid with others, something I will discuss at length in Chapter 4.

For now, I want to spend a minute or two discussing some of the rule-out conditions utilized by both the DSM-5 and researchers when diagnosing and treating SAD in children. As I mentioned earlier, SAD has one of the earliest onset ages of mental disorders. Based on the criteria highlighted within this chapter, it is easy to imagine that misdiagnoses or overdiagnoses could happen. It is important to consider the context of the child's behavior with reference to the potential for social anxiety, as well as the specific development of the child (Beidel & Turner, 2007).

Context of behavior refers to the environment in which the behavior occurs. It is not unusual, for example, for children to be reticent when forced to speak with authority figures. How many of your children readily self-advocate or engage the principal in an in-depth conversation? Not many, right? Considering the context would mean taking a look at the specific situation in which the behaviors of concern occur and where they do not occur. In the case of a child with potential for SAD, the fear-based behaviors must occur within a peer setting, not just with adult interactions. The child with social anxiety will typically interact well with familiar peers, but may become markedly withdrawn or reclusive when forced to interact at school or in specific settings.

In addition to context, specific development of the child must also be considered. The child needs to have demonstrated the capacity to build appropriate social relationships in familiar settings and/or with familiar people. If a child has not demonstrated such capacity, it is unlikely that the social competency challenges are related to social anxiety. In this case, the behaviors are more likely related to cases of social communication deficits, autism spectrum disorders, or similar concerns.

As mentioned previously, other rule-out considerations highlighted by the DSM-5 include duration and comorbidity, both discussed earlier in the chapter.

A Word About Shyness

You'll notice that the term *shy* is used in the title of this book. The reason for this may be different than you think. Most teachers and parents see their children's shyness as something that exists on a continuum, one that eventually leads to social anxiety. The truth is actually much more complicated, and one that must be understood fully in order to best support children suffering with SAD.

Shyness is typically defined in research journals as discomfort in social situations (Henderson & Zimbardo, 1998). Although children with SAD certainly feel discomfort, the reasoning behind the discomfort is different. Support for this point of view can be found in recent studies that indicate that many shy individuals do not simultaneously meet criteria for SAD (Heiser, Turner, & Beidel, 2003; Stein & Stein, 2008).

Many researchers consider shyness a temperament or feature of personality. It is frequently confused with introversion and viewed as something warranting intervention. I consider shyness more of a behavior that can be shaped and changed, something I discuss at length in my book, *Quiet Kids* (Fonseca, 2014). Temperament, including introversion, is part of a person's hardwiring and an aspect of personality. It is neither good nor bad. I will discuss the overlap between shyness, introversion, and social anxiety more in Chapter 2, including illustrating the differences between the three in Tip Sheet #3 (see p. 35). For now, it is simply important to understand that all three are different. Furthermore, all three conditions will benefit from many of the strategies and interventions throughout this book.

GIFTEDNESS, OVEREXCITABILITY, AND SAD

Giftedness is more than scoring high on an intelligence test or earning easy A's in school. It is a term of potential that influences all areas of functioning, including emotional development. Gifted individuals are typically more intense in their emotional responses to their environments, resulting in behaviors that resemble a variety of mental health conditions including SAD (Fonseca, 2011).

Part of the reason for the intense reactions involves Polish psychologist Kazimierz Dabrowski's Theory of Positive Disintegration and Overexcitability. He postulated that gifted individuals were more sensitive and intense in their interactions with their environment. Dabrowski identified five areas of overexcitability, including psychomotor, cognitive, emotional, imaginational, and sensual. Most of the confusion regarding gifted individuals and their behaviors can be clarified by looking more closely at these areas, particularly emotional overexcitability. Defined as extremely emotional reactions to various stimuli, including external stimuli, memories, and thoughts, emotional overexcitability or intensity often results in significant mood swings, anxious behaviors, negation, and avoidance (Probst, 2007).

Sound familiar? Gifted children often engage in significant levels of anxiety and avoidance, especially in response to perceptions of poor performance and anticipation of the same—just like children who are socially anxious.

So how does a parent begin to decipher the social anxiety disorder from the giftedness? At what point should additional assistance be sought? For me, the answer lies in the levels of support being offered to the gifted child. Start with supporting the environment and teaching basic strategies for dealing with performance-related anxiety and social competency. Tip Sheet #1 can provide a few suggestions.

Once support is provided and habituated into the child's routine, look at your child's current behavior. Is he or she continuing to avoid social situations with peers due to fear of humiliation or embarrassment? Is the level of social

Tip Sheet #1

Supporting Emotional Intensity

Emotional Intensity Characteristics	Why This Is a Problem	Intervention
Extreme emotions: Very positive, very negative, or cycling from one to the other	• Emotionally volatile • Child may struggle with managing emotions • Easily misinterpreted as a mood disorder or other emotional problem	• Teach your child how to recognize and manage his or her emotions • Learn the warning signs of your child's escalation cycle • Teach your child how to relax
Extreme empathy with others	• May react (cry, etc.) to others • Will take on the problems of others • Trouble differentiating his or her own emotions	• Teach discernment—how to tell the source of the emotions • Teach that intense emotions is normal part of gifted development • Teach relaxation techniques
Physical symptoms including headache, stomachache, heart palpitations	• Frequently misunderstood as indications of stress or anxiety • Can result in misdiagnoses and inappropriate medical management	• Use biofeedback and similar techniques to help manage physical symptoms • Teach relaxation and meditations • Emphasize healthy lifestyle choices
Inhibition—timidity and shyness	• May be seen as social anxiety • Will appear aloof to others	• Teach how to manage stress • If the child is introverted, care for the introversion first • Address the shyness through practicing how to engage socially

TIP SHEET #1, CONTINUED

Emotional Intensity Characteristics	Why This Is a Problem	Intervention
Strong affective memory—remembering both events *and* the emotions	• May struggle with rumination over past intense events • May struggle with adapting and/or resiliency • May be misunderstood as PTSD-like symptoms	• Focus on healthy living and relaxation • Teach discernment and positive self-talk • Help child understand and embrace emotional intensity
Increased fears and anxieties, existential depression, thoughts of mortality and death	• May appear anxious or depressed • May appear morbid in thought patterns • Often wrestling with existential thoughts at very young age	• Help your child find meaning in life • Align child with like-minded individuals to assist with meaning • Talk openly about fears and questions • Teach relaxation and discernment
Difficulties transitioning and/or adjusting to change	• May appear to have rigid thinking • Difficulty managing emotions during periods of change • May demonstrate decreased resiliency	• Prepare for change ahead of time • Give some autonomy regarding transition to child • Focus on building resiliency and seeing the E.I. as "normal"
Feelings of inadequacy and critical self-evaluations	• Reduction in willingness to take academic risks • Reduction in practice of various social skills, leading to actual inadequacy • Increased depressive symptoms	• Focus on effort over achievement • Teach child to see successes • Teach discernment and correct faulty thinking

Note. Adapted from Emotional Intensity in Gifted Students by C. Fonseca, 2011, Waco, TX: Prufrock Press.

stress prohibiting the child from participating in a variety of activities, school, or previously enjoyed events? If a child is still exhibiting significant anxiety after multiple supports have been offered, then it may be time to consult with a therapist. Just make sure the therapist is familiar with the unique profile of gifted children, including overexcitability and asynchronous development.

Chalk Talk: When Anxiety Comes to School

Social anxiety does not happen without the "social" part. And few places are more social than school. Between the hazards of gym class, the expectation of giving presentations and the social minefield of lunch, children with social anxiety disorder are confronted with the terror behind their disorder for the majority of their school day. Whether they had a previously humiliating experience at school or they are just anticipating problems, students with SAD often suffer in silence or refuse to attend school completely.

Educators are not trained to handle the complexities of students with mental health challenges within their programs. Most of their limited knowledge is learned in the trenches, experimenting with interventions in an often desperate attempt to help. With a disorder as common as SAD, the lack of knowledge can adversely impact many children.

Social anxiety disorder most typically manifests as performance-related anxiety in school. Students with SAD will often withdraw from class, refuse to participate or ask questions (even when they are confused), hide during lunch or recess, and do anything they can to remain unnoticed. Unlike the child with generalized anxiety disorder or other mental health concerns, the SAD child engages in these behaviors in response to the specific social situations in which he or she perceives there to be a high risk of humiliation. The child may appear "fine" in one class, and unable to attend a different class. She may be fine with her friends at lunch, but suffer to the point of avoidance in P.E. Regardless of how the symptoms of SAD are presenting with the school setting, these children often require significant levels of support in order to reduce the negative impact of the school setting and reengage in their learning. Tip Sheet #2 includes several

Tip Sheet #2
Supporting SAD at School

Social Anxiety Triggers	Intervention
Being called on in class	• Don't call on the anxious child unless he or she raises his or her hand • To help build the child's positive experiences, call on the child when you think the answer is likely to be correct, before teaching the child to take risks; encourage risk taking after a few successful attempts at answering questions has been accomplished • Avoid putting the child "on the spot"
New classroom/school	• Encourage the child to visit the school before school is in session • Pair up with one student for a class tour • Establish safe zones for the student • *Note.* It is important to transition safety to the school quickly; this means the parent should likely not accompany the child after the first meeting
Being watched by others	• Allow the child to work with one student or the teacher first; when comfort levels increase, increase the number of people involved • Avoid putting the student "on the spot" whenever possible • Teach the student how to relax
Making "small talk" at recess, in class, or anywhere at school	• Use structured team activities to support all students' learning about how to engage in conversations • Teach the specific skill of making friends and/or initiating and engaging in conversations
Meeting the teacher or principal or other "authority" figures	• Take care not to overwhelm the student with multiple meetings too soon • Take a quiet, gentle approach with the student initially
Speaking to a group or the class	• Start with presenting to one person, then increase to more as the child is able • Teach relaxation techniques • Allow for relaxation breaks before or after performance demands

TIP SHEET #2, CONTINUED

Social Anxiety Triggers	Intervention
Using the restroom at school	• Teach the child where the restrooms are located and when they can be used • If the child is very afraid of the public restrooms, allow him or her to use one in the nurse's office until the fear is reduced • Try to ascertain why the child is afraid and address the specific fear
Performing or speaking in class	• Start with a small group (2+) first, slowly building to large-group presentations • Teach the class to engage in appropriate behavior during presentations • Practice with the student prior to the presentation or performance • Teach relaxation techniques

interventions that can be utilized within the school setting. Try a few of them the next time you have a student you suspect is wrestling with social anxiety.

MEET KAIT

I first met Kait when she wandered into my office as a junior after completing a lengthy stay at a residential placement facility due to significant anxiety and suicidal ideations. I worked with Kait for just longer than a year. Kait was identified as gifted in second grade. She struggled with anxiety-related behaviors throughout elementary school and middle school until she attempted suicide during her sophomore year. She had received counseling, medications, and a variety of therapies prior to her hospitalization. Her story highlights some of the complexities encountered with children who are naturally intense related to giftedness, introversion, and significant anxiety in social situations.

KAIT'S STORY

Kait was a typical bright child: excited about learning, creative, and full of life. That is until she figured out that most kids were not like her. It happened early for Kait; by fourth grade, she knew she wasn't like the other kids in her class. Worse, the kids knew she was different too. They teased her about being smart, made fun of her social awkwardness, and relentlessly excluded her from social outings.

Her elementary teachers didn't really understand Kait. From their perspective, she was a wonderful, dedicated student who was clearly smart and had a bright future. They did not see the other kids exclude Kait from activities; they didn't recognize the subtle ways Kait tried to withdraw from school.

By sixth grade, Kait hated school. She fought with her parents every morning, pretending to be sick just to avoid going to school. Unsure of how to help, her parents took her to the doctor every time Kait said she felt ill. Test after test confirmed what her parents already knew—there was nothing medically wrong with her.

Kait spent her middle school years becoming more and more socially isolated. Given her natural introversion, she liked the solitude at first. Eventually, however, the need to connect became too strong to ignore. Kait struggled to make friendships in real life, so she turned to the Internet to meet her need to connect. Experiencing both emotional and imaginative intensity to a great degree, Kait began to engage in a series of fantasies involving various celebrities online. She stalked their websites and fan sites, connected with like-minded people on those sites, and allowed the fantasy to blossom and consume her.

Cut off from the real world and refusing to attend school on a near-daily basis, Kait was headed for disaster. Her parents took her to therapists and doctors, desperate for answers and help. She was given a variety of diagnoses and placed on various medications. Nothing worked in the end.

Within a year, Kait was in crisis. No longer able to function socially in real life, and restricted from any connections online due to her maladaptive behaviors, Kait decided to try to take her life. She swallowed too many pills and prayed for a quick end that never came. Her stepmother interrupted the attempt, called 911, and Kait was placed in a residential care facility for several months.

Once Kait was released, she transferred to a smaller, alternative school setting to complete her final years of high school. Assessments indicated not only the anxiety, but also significant giftedness, introversion, and several areas of overexcitability. Additional supports were provided, including curriculum adjustments, school-based counseling to address both her giftedness and her social anxiety, and behavioral supports for her overexcitability areas and anxiety. The small school setting was beneficial to Kait. The supports she received, including social skills training, individual counseling at school, private counseling, and ongoing medical management of her now-diagnosed social anxiety disorder worked together to provide Kait with the layers of support she needed in order to function at school.

Kait went on to complete her high school education, seldom missing more than a day or two from school per month. She required significant supports in order to maintain her functioning at school, but responded well to these interventions.

LESSONS LEARNED

As stated earlier, Kait's story is a great lesson in the difficulties of addressing the complex and overlapping needs of giftedness, introversion, and social anxiety. I doubt Kait was destined to become socially anxious. Rather, her story is a cautionary tale of how social anxiety can develop due to a lack of understanding and support. Kait struggled with her social competencies early in school, something typical within the asynchronous development of many gifted children. Interventions at that time, as well as increased support during the episodes of relational aggression, may have resulted in a different outcome, including the avoidance of her mental health crisis.

That said, it is important that we avoid playing Monday morning quarterback, and instead look at her story as a reminder to pay attention to the subtle cues our children give us when they are under significant stress and struggling. Parents are often the first to notice when children are at risk. Working together with educators, many of Kait's experiences throughout elementary and middle school may have been avoided.

Concluding Thoughts

Anxiety disorders in children, and social anxiety in particular are not a new concept. The constructs of social withdrawal and avoidance have existed since the time of Hippocrates. Yet there is much about the dis-

order and effective treatments we still do not understand. This chapter hopefully shed a few rays of light on the symptoms and complexities of the disorder itself, as well as a brief discussion of what social anxiety is not. The next few chapters will examine the biological and environmental factors that can cause and maintain SAD, as well as proactive strategies parents can use to minimize the impact of these factors.

CHAPTER 2

The Biology
of Anxiety

"My son is incredibly self conscious and has been since he was very young, possibly as a result of a diagnosis of verbal dyspraxia (with associated speech difficulties) and a high IQ which may have exacerbated his self-consciousness. He avoids new social occasions and becomes anxious at even the thought of having to make conversation outside of the normal interactions he has (e.g., telling his teacher that he has to leave early for an appointment)." —Parent of gifted child wrestling with social anxiety

Much of the current research in the mental health field centers on the biological and neurological factors influencing the development of various mental health illnesses, including anxiety and depression. Biological factors, in fact, are a well-accepted predisposing factor within the etiological models of social anxiety disorder. That said, our understanding of the brain and the neurobiological aspects of emotion and mental health is still in its infancy. This chapter examines the current research while acknowledging that there is more unknown than known when it comes to fully understanding the impact of neurobiological factors on the development of anxiety disorders, including social anxiety disorder.

General Science of Anxiety and Fear

Before we can discuss the general physiological aspects of both fear and anxiety, it is helpful to have common definitions of both terms.

Although highly debated within the scientific community, most researchers generally define fear as an *immediate* emotion linked to our fight-or-flight response. Anxiety, however, is routed in the *anticipation* of future events that are thought to bring about fear or a negative response (Barlow, 2004). To further clarify, Barlow (2004) defined anxious apprehension as a cyclical response to threats in which the trigger of a threat (i.e., a facial expression or in the case of social anxiety, a request to perform socially) leads to a shifting and narrowing of attention to be more self-involved, resulting in increased negation, which in turn negatively reinforces the anticipated threat. And on and on the cycle goes.

I find this differentiation between an actual real-time event versus something that is anticipated important. It points to the inherent nature of anxiety as being grounded in the future, in the "thought" of what may occur, as opposed to being grounded in reality. The emphasis of the cyclical nature of the anticipation is also important in that it is indicative of how habitual anxiety can become when it is not addressed and redirected.

Most researchers agree that the emotions of both fear and anxiety biologically involve two key structures in the brain: the amygdala and the prefrontal cortex, both of which are involved in the brain's "fear circuit" (Robertson-Nay & Brown, 2011). The amygdala is involved in the processing of emotions and memory. The amygdala and prefrontal cortex combine to process threat information, with the amygala processing immediate threats (Phillips, Drevets, Rauch, & Lane, 2003), and the prefrontal cortex more involved with delayed processing of emotional regulation (Hariri, Mattay, Tessitore, Fera, & Weinberger, 2003). Animal research confirms the involvement of both the amygdala and the prefrontal cortex in social anxiety and the processing of social threats (Brühl, Delsignore, Komossa, & Weidt, 2014; Robertson-Nay & Brown, 2011). Research points to the engagement of the amygdala in response to social threat cues, especially facial cues, as being key in the understanding of social anxiety (Bogels et al., 2010).

Another aspect of neurobiology and social anxiety worth mentioning involves the neurotransmitter dopamine. Dopamine is linked to the pleasure and reward centers of the brain. It also is involved with mood regulation and decision making. Low dopamine levels have been linked with everything from Parkinson's disease to addiction. There is significant evidence that low dopamine activity may also be linked to social anxiety disorder (Schneier et al., 2000; Freitas-Ferrari et al., 2010). Interestingly, a low dopamine preference has also been indicated in introverted temperaments (Laney, 2002), something addressed later in this chapter.

Before you start having flashbacks of your college biology class, let me answer the question I am certain is on your mind: What does all of this amygdala, prefrontal cortex, and dopamine stuff mean? It means that the structure and chemistry of our brains, in particular, the functioning of our amygdalas and utilization of dopamine, heavily influences how we perceive and respond to threats. And it is precisely our perception of threat that determines the scope and depth of our anxiety.

Worksheet #3 is one tool you can use with yourself or your children to help determine whether or not the social anxiety is related to an immediate concern or the anticipation of something that hasn't yet occured. Learning to self-reflect and differentiate between a real-time threat and an anticipated threat is the first step toward helping your children manage their anxiety response (Heitmann et al., 2014).

Temperament and Behavior Inhibition

In addition to the predisposing factors involving the amygdala, the prefrontal cortex and dopamine, researchers continue to look at temperament as a possible predictor of social anxiety disorder. Temperament is typical defined as the biologically based human traits that influence emotional, behavioral, and social development (Fonseca, 2014). It is constant in nature, remaining largely unchanged over a lifetime.

One aspect of temperament that has received a lot of attention from researchers looking for the biological basis of anxiety disorders is behavior inhibition, or BI. Defined in the research as avoidance, shyness, social discomfort, and the fear of unfamiliar situations (Kagan, 1989), behavior inhibition is considered a predisposing and/or additive factor for the developmental of anxiety disorders, including SAD (Broeren, Newall, Dodd, Locker, & Hudson, 2014; Higa-McMillan & Ebesutani, 2011).

Some researchers have identified two components of BI, including a physical threat component and a social threat component. Although

Worksheet #3

Threat Discernment

Directions: Read and answer each question as it relates to the specific situation.

1. What is the specific event you are anxious about?

   _____
   _____
   _____
   _____
   _____
   _____

2. What proof can you find that your fears are justified?

   _____
   _____
   _____
   _____
   _____
   _____

3. Now that you KNOW something and are not ASSUMING, what can you do to change the outcome (if you want to)? Be specific.

   _____
   _____
   _____
   _____
   _____
   _____

4. If you discovered that your original ideas were incorrect in some way, how can you change them? What are your new ideas?

   _____
   _____
   _____
   _____
   _____
   _____

physical threat does not appear to be related to later development of SAD, social threat does. Additionally, social threats that occur in childhood and the resultant behavior inhibition are also found to be linked to depression (Higa-McMillan & Ebesutani, 2011).

So what does this all mean? Children who exhibit behavioral inhibition may be at increased risk for the development of SAD, especially if the behavioral inhibition has been linked to social threats or perceived social threats. I will talk more about threats, real and perceived, in the next chapter. For now, the important take-away message is the impact of behavior inhibition on the development of social anxiety.

Before we discuss how to determine if your child is exhibiting BI, I think it is important to address the apparent commonalities between behavioral inhibition and introversion. Introversion, a specific temperament defined by Jung (1971) as someone who fundamentally seeks internal stimulation, is a term often given to individuals who are socially withdrawn and shy. That is an inaccurate use of the word. Many introverts are not so much socially withdrawn, as much as they prefer quiet solitude to the emotionally draining environment of a loud classroom or party. Furthermore, introverts are able to develop friendships, can often perform in front of an audience, and function comfortably within highly social arenas for short periods of time (Fonseca, 2014). That does not sound quite the same as the child experiencing behavior inhibition or social anxiety disorder. Tip Sheet #3 (see p. 35) can further clarify some of the attributes separating shyness, introversion, and behavioral inhibition.

We've established that there is a link between behavioral inhibition and later development of social anxiety disorder. And we've established that not all cases of shyness or social avoidance are actual cases of behavioral inhibition. How can you, as a parent, begin to differentiate your child's behavior and offer support? It starts with looking at the root causes of the behavior, when you first began to identify the behavior and the environments in which you see the avoidance occur. Questionnaire #3 can help you begin to untangle the complicated threads of behavior to help determine what may really be happening with your child. Chapter 9 will help you utilize the information gleaned from this questionnaire and develop specific supports for your child.

Questionnaire #3

Shyness, Avoidance, or Behavior Inhibition?

Directions: Read each statement and decide if it is true for your child all of the time, some of the time, or none of the time. Check the appropriate box. When you have completed the questionnaire, have your child complete a separate questionnaire. Add up the totals for each and compare the results.

	All	Some	None
I get nervous before a speaking event.			
I think about an upcoming speaking event for weeks or months ahead of time, imagining all of the ways it can go wrong.			
I get nervous and stressed when meeting new people.			
Whenever I have to meet new people, I automatically assume they are going to laugh at me or find me socially awkward.			
I am immediately nervous when the teacher calls on me in class.			
I stay nervous long after the teacher has called on me, replaying the encounter and looking for all of the ways I answered incorrectly.			
I will avoid going to a party just to avoid the potential for humiliation or embarrassment.			
I get nervous when attending unfamiliar events, but I can usually manage my fear.			
I get so nervous when attending unfamiliar events that I can't think clearly and will often try to find ways to avoid the event all together.			
I worry when taking a test so much that I am thinking about the test for days or weeks ahead of time, nearly panicking.			

Total your responses. List the "all" statements on the lines below. These statements are indications that your shyness and/or avoidance may be more than simply feeling shy. Jot down any particular areas of concern.

_____

_____

Is It Genetic?

This chapter has focused a lot on neurological and physiological aspects of social anxiety disorder. The question that frequently comes at this point involves genetics and the inheritability of the biological precursors of social anxiety disorder. In layman terms, is social anxiety inheritable?

Researchers are not in agreement regarding the presence of a genetic link influencing the development of social anxiety. Introversion, behavioral inhibition, and even the fear of a negative response have been found to be inheritable (Higa-McMillan & Ebesutani, 2011). However there is little consistent evidence linking SAD to a specific genetic link. Instead there are broad genetic tendencies that appear to be related and common to SAD (Bogels et al., 2010).

Anecdotal evidence from my own practice, as well as a common opinion among clincians indicates a strong liklihood that SAD runs within family units. Whether this is strictly due to physiological factors is unclear. Regardless, it does appear that anxious parents yield anxious children, something I discuss further in Chapter 3.

INTROVERSION, SHYNESS, OR BEHAVIOR INHIBITION

As I mentioned earlier, there is a lot of overlap within introversion, shyness, and the behavior inhibition often associated with social anxiety disorder. Based on both research and my professional experiences, shyness is an overused term that has come to be used interchangeably with both introversion and behavior inhibition. It has even been suggested that shyness is merely a less extreme version of social anxiety. Although this appears true on the surface, the truth is significantly more complicated. Shyness is a behavior, initially initiated in response to the behavioral inhibition sometimes found with introversion. That behavior is reinforced and can easily become habit. Behavioral inhibition is closely related to shyness and relates to a person's reaction to both physical and social threats. Introversion is a specific type of temperament related to a specific way of utilizing energy and renewal.

To help differentiate between the terms, I have developed a chart comparing the features of shyness, introversion, and behavior inhibition. Tip Sheet #3 identifies many of the specific features of each term. The strategies in this book can help with the more problematic outcomes of all three of these aspects of behavior and temperament.

Tip Sheet #3 makes it clear that being withdrawn or avoidant of social situations can happen for many reasons. This behavior does not determine social anxiety, although it can function as a predictor of potential social anxiety. The development of an anxiety disorder, especially social anxiety, happens over time and is often due to several interconnected factors. Temperament is only one aspect of the total picture.

Chalk Talk: Social Anxiety Versus Shyness— When to Push and When to Back Off

Teachers see it every year: students who avoid social contact, divert their eyes during class discussions, and withdraw from social situations at lunch and break. Most of the time, the behavior happens early in the year. Teachers cajole and coax the "shy" student to make friends, participate in class, and climb out of his or her shell. And most of the time, it works.

But not always.

Sometimes the behavior teachers assume is a matter of normal shyness or apprehension is really the warning signs of social anxiety. In these cases, each moment of effort to coax and cajole the student to comply with required engagement can result in increased avoidance behaviors. Eventually, the student may even withdraw completely from the class or school environment, something neither the teacher nor the parent wants to happen.

So how can the teacher know when the behavior he is observing is a matter of "normal" start-of-the-school year jitters versus something more serious? First, start with the parent. Ask if the child has demonstrated similar avoidant behavior in other situations or at other times. Talk with previous teachers and spend a lot of time observing the student. Take a soft approach, always trying to set the student up for early success.

Tip Sheet #3

Shyness, Introversion, and Behavior Inhibition

Event	What the Shy Child Says	What the Child With Behavior Inhibition Says	What the Introverted Child Says
The first day at a new school	"I am nervous I won't make any friends. But I am going to try to make it a good day, even though my stomach hurts."	"I can't do this. People are going to laugh at me when I don't know what to do or where to go. I just know this is going to be the worst day ever."	"This is a bit scary. I am going to watch what other people do so I can learn the social rules here. After school, I am spending time alone to recharge."
Attending a large party	"I really should go to this party. People expect me to be there. Never mind that I feel like throwing up. I know I will be miserable and afraid, but maybe I can suck it up and go anyway."	"All of those people are going to look at me all night, waiting for me to act stupid. And we all know, I WILL act stupid eventually. Better to not go than risk the humiliation."	"There is no way I am going to such a large party. It just takes too much of my energy. I'll meet up with a few friends after the party."
Refuses to call a close friend on the telephone.	"I never know what to say on the phone, so I am just going to text him."	"I hate calling people, having them expect me to be a certain way over the phone. I don't really need to talk to him. I can wait."	"Yeah, I don't call. Too emotionally draining. I text though. All the time. No problems with that at all. In truth, I love connecting and texting lets me do it without the energy suck."

TIP SHEET #3, CONTINUED

Event	What the Shy Child Says	What the Child With Behavior Inhibition Says	What the Introverted Child Says
Participating in a small group in class	"I wonder if my group mates will laugh at me. I hope not. Maybe if one of my friends are with me I can do it."	"These people are waiting for me to fail. I can just picture it—in 2 weeks, when we break into groups, they are going to laugh at me, stare at me, watch me humiliate myself. Nope, I can't let that happen. I'm going to skip school."	"Small groups aren't so bad. I hope there aren't a bunch of high-energy extroverts—they are exhausting to be around. All of the noise and chatter and movement. Ugh."
Sitting alone at lunch instead of joining a nearby group	"I never know what to say to others. That group looks nice, but I just can't get up the courage to join them."	"I don't feel good. Seriously, I think I might have a panic attack just think-ing about joining a group with people I don't really know. At least if I avoid them I can avoid a little embarrassment."	"Finally, a moment of solitude and peace. YES! I am so happy to just have a quick moment of stillness."
Being called on in class	"I always get nervous when Ms. Jones starts calling on people. What if she calls on me? What if I don't know the answer? I better just look away and hope she doesn't say my name."	"No way am I staying in this class when I know she's going to call on me and embarrass me. If I ask to go to the bath-room, maybe I can avoid this. Better yet, if I ditch the class all together I won't have to risk being called on at all."	"Now that I am com-fortable, I am happy to participate in class. After all, I know the answers most of the time."

Tip Sheet #4

When Should I Push?

First, ask yourself the following questions related to classroom expectations and performance:

1. What do I want the child to do?
2. Keeping in mind the specific activity, answer the following questions:
   o Is this activity critical to the curriculum?
   o Will altering the performance/mastery demonstration expectations of the task inhibit the student's growth or alter the goal of the task?
   o Is the student in distress?
   o Am I in a power struggle with the child?
   o What is the worst thing that will happen if I push the child? If I back off?
   o Is the activity worth it?

Use these questions anytime you begin to question whether or not you should push the student harder.

Praise the student when he or she is able to participate, but don't call a lot of attention to him or her. The idea is to normalize the social aspects of school and performance expectations so that the anxious student no longer perceives those events as a threat.

Tip Sheet #4 includes a series of questions and indicators to assist teachers in knowing when it is time to push and when it is time to pull back. Ultimately, the child's behavior is the first, best indicator of the impact of your specific intervention. If the child is in distress, or if his or her distress increases, it is clearly time to pull back and regroup. Most children will not fake a case of anxiety. And although an anxious response can be habitual, that does not make it less real or less "valid" to the child.

MEET JACOB

Jacob and I met when he was a sixth-grade student. His mother came to me at the start of the school year, scared as many parents are about the transition into middle school. She told me that Jacob had been recently diagnosed with fibromyalgia and was at risk for ulcers. She also told me that Jacob's doctor was concerned that the real problem was "in his head." Jacob had a family history of generalized anxiety disorder (GAD) and depression and his mother was concerned that the behaviors were indicative of mental health problems with Jacob.

Jacob and I started meeting weekly for just over a year, and then monthly throughout middle school. Jacob received regular medical care for his medical diagnoses. His parents had unsuccessfully tried therapy a year before he started in middle school. Jacob had a history of inconsistent school attendance related to his medical issues and the pain he reported to his mother.

I wanted to include Jacob's story because it highlights the mind-body connection and what can happen when social anxiety is untreated. As with the other stories, Jacob is just one example of the connection between physical, mental, and emotional health.

JACOB'S STORY

Jacob came to our first session dressed in jeans, a T-shirt, and a hoodie with the hood covering his face, despite the near-100-degree day. He spoke little more than single-word answers to my questions that day. It was a pattern that repeated for 6 weeks until he had a severely sore stomach and sought my help.

The pain had been triggered by a test, something he later reported as common. He described the feeling as though acid was eating through his gut. I walked him through a few breathing exercises until he was stable, the pain had subsided, and we were able to just talk. That moment, when he allowed me to walk through his pain with him, was our turning point. From that moment on, Jacob was a willing participant in each and every session.

His story started long before middle school, however. Jacob reported that he never wanted to attend school. His mother shared that same belief, explaining the hours of crying that precipitated the first days of kindergarten. He cried when she dropped him off, cried during the school day, and cried when he got home.

Nothing seemed to ease the separation anxiety for Jacob, and so the painful mornings continued for the entire year.

First grade was better. Jacob met someone new on the first day of class and a friendship developed. As long as his friend was at school, Jacob would leave his mother's side. But on the days the boy was sick, Jacob still struggled.

By fourth grade, Jacob's attendance mirrored his friend's. He no longer cried when he left his mother, but he withdrew from most of his peers and was considered a reluctant learner by his teachers.

At the end of fourth grade, Jacob's friend moved away, sending Jacob in a tailspin. Although he no longer cried, he began to develop physical symptoms that created a barrier to school attendance. He complained of severe stomach pains, experienced significant bouts of vomiting and diarrhea, and severe reflux problems. Additionally, Jacob complained of significant pain in his joints and legs, as well as chronic and unexplained headaches.

Jacob's parents took him to the doctor and a diagnosis of fibromyalgia was made. The doctor recommended dietary and medication regimes, as well as therapy to address what he felt were underlying anxiety-related concerns.

Jacob refused most treatment options and continued to struggle with his health and school attendance. Additionally, he struggled at home, often withdrawing from friends and family, citing his chronic pain as the reason for his inability to interact socially. By the time Jacob started sixth grade, he was receiving school support through a Section 504 plan that included support to help him get caught up after being absent, a "safe place" to go when he was feeling scared or anxious, and counseling with the school psychologist. The supports were only marginally effective at the start of sixth grade, as Jacob continued to struggle with school attendance and engagement in peer interactions.

My work with Jacob focused on two things: increasing body awareness with a goal of being able to adjust his physical reaction to stress and developing a vocabulary to talk about his fears and/or triggers.

Jacob had the most success with his vocabulary and communication skills (see Tip Sheet #5). He learned ways to communicate to his parents and one or two people at school when he was feeling overwhelmed. In fact, Jacob used the word *overwhelmed* to indicate any anxious feeling. When he had a test or even just a class environment that he struggled with, he would quietly tell the teacher he was overwhelmed. He was allowed to leave the class, go to a safe place, and decompress for a bit before returning to class. This word

Tip Sheet #5

Building an Emotional Vocabulary

- Work within the developmental age of your child.
- Choose words that can cue the child about his or her emotional state.
- Choose the words together.
- Make sure everyone agrees on the meanings of the words chosen.
- Draw pictures and/or make cards for the emotional vocabulary.
- Encourage using the new emotional vocabulary on a consistent basis.

became a primary way Jacob could communicate the feeling of panic he felt prior to a full case if anxiety taking hold. Other phrases Jacob used were "too much," "need to breathe," and "need a break."

Jacob's development of a specialized vocabulary specifically for his stress and anxiety put him in charge of his world, and that autonomy served to reduce his stressors and triggers. The more confident he began to feel, the more he was able to manage his physical reactions to his environment. It was a slow process, but Jacob had a lot of success during his middle school years.

Unfortunately, things changed as he transitioned into high school and adolescence. Increased social demands overwhelmed his fragile coping system, and Jacob returned to his previous pattern of responding to stress, resulting in the development of social phobias. But not all of the progress made in middle school was lost. His positive experiences in school-based counseling opened the door to more intensive therapy. Jacob began working with a mental health team, partnering medication with therapy. The results were positive and within 2 years, Jacob was able to consistently attend school. Furthermore, by his senior year, he had developed a few closer peer relationships and made plans to go away to school, something he was unable to consider a few years prior.

LESSONS LEARNED

Jacob's medical condition was intrinsically linked to his social anxiety. This is not unique. Many students with significant anxiety report similar physical symptoms associated with their anxiety, almost as though they literally inhale their stress. Unfortunately, though, as the physical symptoms appear, treatment is often limited to the body, without extending to the mental health component.

Jacob's story is a reminder that the underlying anxiety, clearly present from early school experiences and likely related to genetic factors, must be addressed in order to improve overall outcomes. In Jacob's case, the medical symptoms could not be adequately managed without Jacob learning specific strategies to identify and reduce his internal levels of stress. Furthermore, teaching Jacob about the physical aspects of his particular stress—the ways his body demonstrated heightened states of arousal—served to enable Jacob to regain some control and autonomy over his world. This improved perception of mastery is, in my opinion, what ultimately led to later improvements in Jacob's overall functioning. Worksheet #4 will allow you to use this same strategy with your child.

Concluding Thoughts

Social anxiety is a complicated disorder, with numerous predisposing factors that can make a person more susceptible to developing the disorder. Many of these factors have a physiological basis. Changes in dopamine utilization, as seen with some introverts, as well as activation of the amygdala and prefrontal cortex can all predispose a child to the development of social anxiety. But it takes more than simple biology to create an anxious child. It is the combination of a child's biology along with environmental factors that will often lead to that first significant crisis that can later develop into SAD.

The next chapter will look at many of the environmental factors that lead to SAD and their connection to the neurological foundations discussed here.

Worksheet #4

Understanding My Stress

Directions: Following the example and the information from Worksheet #2: My Early Warning Signs (p. 13), complete the following chart about your stress cycle.

Steps	Physical Signs (How does your body feel? What areas are tense?)	Emotional Signs (How do you feel? What is your emotional state?)
First: Initial sign that something is bothering you	*Example: My hands begin to sweat and my breathing becomes shallow* • _____ • _____ • _____ • _____	*Example: I begin to feel like I'm in danger* • _____ • _____ • _____
Second: If you continue to escalate, what happens?	*Example: I feel the walls closing in on me and like I am suffocating* • _____ • _____ • _____ • _____	*Example: I feel like I have to leave immediately* • _____ • _____ • _____
Third: When you are at your highest point of stress, what happens?	*Example: I can't think, so I scream and leave* • _____ • _____ • _____ • _____	*Example: I am in a panic; nothing makes sense to me and I can't force myself to stop* • _____ • _____ • _____ • _____
Miscellaneous: Add stages as needed	• _____ • _____ • _____ • _____	• _____ • _____ • _____ • _____

CHAPTER 3

Environmental Causes of Social Anxiety

"My son is 6 years old, and for the past 2 years, he has endured harrowing social anxiety compounded with tendencies toward obsessive-compulsive disorder. His early years of school as well as his involvement in social activities have been greatly impacted. I myself began feeling social anxiety during my senior year of high school when I was 17 years old. I stopped performing in the theater and, though I'd always been shy by nature, I began to avoid anything having to do more than a couple of people. It has persisted for nearly 17 years now.

During a particularly stressful period of my life, I began having severe panic attacks. I didn't know what was wrong with me and I was so terribly frightened that I became agoraphobic, which in turn fed the social anxiety. I stopped leaving my house except to take my children to school, and even then I wore huge sunglasses so the helpers getting my children out of the van in the preschool drop-off line wouldn't see me. I withdrew so far into myself that I barely spoke to some of my closest friends because I didn't know how to talk to them. People I talked to nearly every day were suddenly too intimidating. I went through intensive behavioral modification therapy. It was by far one of the most frightening things I've done. I also went through a medication change. I had the presence of mind to know I did not want to live that way. It did change my life, definitely, but I try hard not to let it define me." —Sarah, adult and parent dealing with social anxiety

Biological predisposition to anxiety isn't the only route to social anxiety disorder. In most cases, a combination of environmental factors leads to the development of SAD. These influences include everything from parenting style and early childhood trauma, to fear conditioning and cognitive bias.

The Impact of Parenting

Anxious parents and parenting styles often result in children with higher levels of anxiety (Higa-McMillan & Ebesutani, 2011). Often anxious parents overemphasize the opinions of others while de-emphasizing the importance of the family. Furthermore, many anxious parents socially isolate the family, further perpetrating a sense of fear with regard to anything "outside" the immediate family structure, setting the stage for the development of socially anxious children.

But why do some parents approach parenting from such an anxious and protective point of view? The answer, I believe, is in both the social-emotional history of the parent and the parenting style experienced.

As stated in the beginning of the book, social anxiety can last throughout a person's life. Furthermore, SAD is often more intense when it develops during childhood (Alfano & Biedel, 2011). It is no surprise, then, that anxious parents result in anxious children. Preventing this anxious cycle requires intervention both for the parent and the child. Questionnaire #4 can help you determine the degree to which your own cognitive biases and anxiety is impacting your parenting style.

As mentioned earlier, there is a clear connection between parenting styles and the potential development of social anxiety disorder. So-called "helicopter" and "tiger" parenting, both characterized by overprotective, rejecting styles, have been connected to the development of SAD both through retrospective questionaires with socially anxious adults (Wood, McLeod, Sigman, Hwang, & Chu, 2003), and through questioning the parents of socially anxious youth (Lieb et al., 2000).

What is it about these particular parenting styles that increase the likelihood of the development and maintenance of SAD? Helicopter parenting is characterized by parents who are highly involved in every aspect of the child's life, often to the point of enabling or "hovering" in and around the child. This specific parenting style often emerges as

Questionnaire #4

My Anxiety and Parenting

Directions: Read each statement and decide if you agree, disagree, or neither agree nor disagree. Check the appropriate box.

	I agree	I disagree	I neither agree nor disagree
I worry my children may be laughed at by others.			
I worry about my kids being embarrassed at school.			
I worry my children will be bullied.			
My fears make me want to intervene on my children's behave.			
I'd rather help my children appear successful than have them be embarrassed.			
I assist my children with homework to make sure they get it done correctly every time.			
I worry about my children's social skills, so I facilitate every social interaction.			
I define my own successes by my children's.			
Seeing my children struggle is very difficult for me to endure.			
I intervene for my children when they struggle.			
I take an active role in solving my children's problems.			
I will often talk to teachers for my children.			
I will often advocate for my children instead of letting them do it themselves.			
People tell me I am overly involved in my children's lives.			
People tell me that I am overprotective. But the world is a very scary place and I need to make sure my children are always safe.			

Once you are finished, reflect on your answers. Can you see ways in which your anxiety can impact your parenting decisions? What do you notice?

_____

_____

_____

_____

_____

_____

_____

_____

_____

_____

_____

_____

_____

_____

_____

_____

_____

_____

_____

_____

_____

_____

_____

_____

_____

_____

a rebound from the typically more aloof style of parenting that occured for many "helicopter" parents. It has also developed in response to a world that is increasingly changing and often more dangerous. Concerns over the economy, the general unrest in the Middle East, public health scares including Ebola and pertussis, as well as recent school shootings and the like have all created a world that feels less safe in many respects. Helicopter parenting was born from a need of parents to cacooon and protect their children. Unfortunately, this parenting style often weakens a child's resiliency, delaying the development of many areas of social competency and eroding the attributes of mastery and social connections, both of which are vital for the development of resiliency. The news is often filled with stories of college recruiters and employers frustrated with milliennials who have been parented by overprotective and overinvolved parents, citing the constant involvement of the parent as a reason to deny college admittance or employment to children.

Researchers have confirmed that the overly protective nature of helicopter parenting often results in children who are significantly more anxious than their counterparts raised with more balanced parenting approaches (Muris, Meesters, Merckelbach, & Hulsenbeck, 2000). Furthermore, studies examining overprotective parenting style indicate a socialization of anxiety in the children that leads to more serious cases of social anxiety (Affrunti & Woodruff-Borden, 2014).

Where helicopter parents protect and enable related to their need to keep their children safe, tiger parents protect and enable related to the need for excellence. Tiger parenting, made famous by self-proclaimed "tiger mom" Amy Chua's book *The Battle Hymn of the Tiger Mother* (2011), is characterized by highly involved parents whose primary goal is for their children to excel in academics with the goal of attending a presitigious college and employment. For the tiger parent, nothing comes before academic performance and family, especially not the distraction of social interactions. Effort is valued less than results. On the surface, this style of parenting appears to result in significant success. Most Tier I colleges, including Harvard and Yale, are filled with children whose parents adopted this style of parenting, demanding excellence in grades and performance from their earliest elementary experiences. However, dig deeper, and it's clear that there is a hefty price to pay for this style of parenting. Because social connections are not valued as highly as achievement, many children lack development of their social competencies. Furthermore, the increased demands for excellence can force a level of perfectionism that increases the likelihood of the development of social anxiety, test anxiety, and generalized anxiety disorder. Recent research with authoritative parenting styles like tiger parenting have demonstrated the connection between overcontrolling, emotionally distant parenting, and social anxiety in children (Bogels, van Oosten, Muris, & Smulders, 2001; Teetsel, Ginsburg, & Drake, 2014).

It is important for parents to learn how to balance instilling a strive for excellence, developing protection factors, and building resiliency within their specific parenting styles. Questionnaire #5 can assist families in determining what their major style of parenting is, their focus, and how to enhance and modify their parenting style to improve child outcomes.

No conversation about parenting and its impact on social anxiety would be complete without taking a moment to discuss early childhood attachment. Different from "bonding" or skin-to-skin connections in early childhood, attachment refers to the early establishment of a connection between the child and a primary caregiver in which the primary caregiver functions as a base or foundation from which the child can explore his or her world and a safety net as needed. There are several types of attachment, including secure, anxious-avoidant insecure, anxious-resistant (or ambivalent) insecure, and disorganized-disoriented (Benoit, 2004), all the result of how the primary caregiver interacts with children in infancy and early childhood. Secure attachment happens when parents respond to their children's needs in a way that is quick and consistent. Anxious-avoidant insecure attachment happens when parents are distant and detached, while anxious-resistant insecure attachment occurs when parents are insensitive, inconsistent, or ambivalent. Disorganized-disoriented attachment occurs in households where the parenting responsiveness to a child's needs is extremely erratic, ranging from frightening to highly neglectful.

Researchers have long identified anxious-resistant attachment as being associated with the development of various anxiety disorders (Higa-McMillan & Ebesutani, 2011). This type of attachment often

Questionnaire #5

What's My Parenting Style?

Directions: Read each statement and decide if you agree, disagree, or neither agree nor disagree. Check the appropriate box.

	I agree	I disagree	I neither agree nor disagree
There are clear expectations for behavior in my house, and the children know what they are.			
Today's world is dangerous. It is my job to protect my children.			
My children need to follow my rules. It is not up for debate.			
My parents were too hard on me, so I am more lenient.			
The most important attitude in our house is respect.			
I think being my children's friend is at least as important as being an authoritative figure.			
My motto is "My way or the highway."			
Having too many rules in the house stifles creativity.			
I treat my children with respect and expect the same from them.			
I need to teach my children everything—it is the only way to keep them safe.			
It is important to me what others think about my children.			
The things my children do are a direct reflection of my parenting—so I have to stay highly involved.			
Guilt is a powerful motivator!			
Being a parent is my most important job.			
My children are too young to make their own decisions about things.			

Once you are finished, reflect on your answers. Using both this tool and Questionnaire #4 (p. 45), what trends do you notice? What aspects of your parenting help build resiliency? What aspects contribute negatively to your child's anxiety?

occurs when the primary caregiver is insensitive to the needs of the child and/or inconsistent (Benoit, 2004). Current research that examines the correlation between attachment and social anxiety disorder has indicated that securely attached children report far less social anxiety than those children whose parents were insensitive, inconsistent, and rejecting, resulting in anxious-resistant and anxious-avoidant attachments (Bohlin, Hagekull, & Rydell, 2000).

The Nature of Fear

Parenting styles and types of attachment aren't the only environmental factors that need to be considered as potential predisposing factors or triggers in the development of social anxiety. The child's response to fear is another large consideration.

Fear is no stranger. It is a basic emotion necessary to our survival as a species. It alerts us to real-time dangers and threats within the environment and tells us when to engage our fight-or-flight response. Without our fear circuit, humanity would have never survived. That said, sometimes our fear circuit gets us into trouble, signaling a threat when no actual threat exists. This is particularly true with socially anxious children and adults.

The fear circuit becomes triggered based on our perception of what constitutes a threat, something we need to fear. For most of us, direct conditioning, or the direct experience of fear, is the major factor influencing our fear circuitry, and in turn sets the stage for the development of anxiety. When children or adults link a specific event to social defeat or humiliation, it sets the stage for the development of social anxiety. This is especially true if similar events yield similar results. In 40%–60% of cases of social anxiety, a direct experience of humiliation or social defeat is a major triggering event (Higa-McMillan & Ebesutani, 2011).

In addition to direct conditioning, our fear response is also influenced by indirect experiences. In these cases, the social defeat or humiliation is observed to happen in another person. For example, imagine that your child is sitting in class with a good friend. Your child witnesses the friend being humiliated by their classmates during an oral presentation.

It is possible that your child will be as traumatized as the friend. She may even be more impacted than her friend. In this scenario, the indirect experience of fear is enough to elicit a response in your child and set up the potential for social anxiety to develop.

Early childhood trauma can also affect our fear responses. Although the research on the connection between exposure to traumatic events and the development of social anxiety is not clear, there is some research to suggest that parental verbal aggression in the home sets the stage for potential SAD in the children (Magee, 1999; Sachs-Ericsson, Verona, Joiner, & Preacher, 2006).

Faulty Thinking

Cognitive bias refers to errors in our thinking characterized by a person's preferential attention, interpretation, and recall of events and information that is consistent with our specific schema (Higa-McMillan & Ebesutani, 2011). In other words, cognitive biases refer to errors in thinking that influence our decision making in order to perpetrate our specific point of view. Faulty thinking is behind many anxiety disorders, including social anxiety. Specifically, the biases of selectively attending to and recalling socially threatening events over neutral events, and interpreting neutral environmental cues as threatening support the socially anxious person to maintain his or her view that the world is a scary place. This, then, maintains his or her anxiety levels. Let's break down these biases a little more specifically.

Human beings are predisposed to pay attention to facial gestures and to associate these nonverbal signals with various emotions (Robertson-Nay & Brown, 2011). Initially, we are somewhat neutral in our attention, acknowledging and discerning between the negative, more threatening emotions and the neutral, nonthreatening ones. However, as our environment shapes our responses, we begin to pay more heightened attention to certain types of facial expressions over others. In the case of social anxiety, increased attention is given to negative facial cues, causing somewhat selective attention being given to things perceived as threatening. Whether this increased attention is related to neurological factors or fear conditioning is uncertain (Higa-McMillan & Ebesutani, 2011). Regardless, the increased attention given to threats serves to increase the anticipatory stress and anxiety. This increased and selective attention also begins to shape our cognitive biases with reference to fear and threats and sets the stage for not only the development of SAD, but the maintenance of the anxiety as well.

Similar to selective attention, socially anxious children and adults often interpret ambiguous social events in negative ways. They assume the most negative outcomes for the event, expect low personal performance within the social situation, and overestimate the impact of the social event to their social status (Miers, Blote, Bogels, & Westenberg, 2008). Their faulty thinking leads them to interpret the most innocent of events in a threatening way, confirming all of their beliefs about why social events should be feared, enhancing their anticipation anxiety, and rooting the social anxiety even deeper.

Cognitive bias is a clear aspect of social anxiety, both enabling the anxiety to develop initially and maintaining it once it appears. It can be hard to break these biases, but not impossible. The first step, however, is understanding the depth to which faulty thinking is impacting both you, as the parent, and your child. Worksheet #5 can help you determine the impact of cogitive bias on you and your children. Later in the book I will address some specific ways to challenge your child's cognitive biases (or your own).

Social Skills and Social Competence

Social competency is typically defined as having the cognitive, emotional, and behavioral skills necessary to adapt and function in our social society. It is developmental in nature, and involves social skills, social awareness, self-confidence, and emotional intelligence (Kostelnik, Gregory, Soderman, & Whiren, 2012).

Children and adults with SAD struggle with all aspects of social competence. From the development and execution of appropriate social skills, to the demonstration of strong prosocial behavior and competent interpretation of our social world (nonverbal cues, facial expressions,

Worksheet #5

Understanding My Beliefs

Directions: This exercise builds on Questionnaire #4 (p. 45). Read each statement and determine if it is true for you, why you feel this way and the impact to your child.

Belief	Agree?	Why?	Impact to child
I worry my children may be laughed at by others.	Yes	Because I was laughed at and children are cruel.	My child believes she will be laughed at most of the time.
I worry about my kids being embarrassed at school.			
I worry my children will be bullied.			
My fears make me want to intervene on my children's behalf.			
I'd rather help my children appear successful than have them be embarrassed.			
I assist my children with homework to make sure they get it done correctly every time.			
I worry about my children's social skills, so I facilitate every social interaction.			
I define my own successes by my children's.			
Seeing my children struggle is very difficult for me to endure.			
I intervene for my children when they struggle.			
I take an active role in solving my children's problems.			

Belief	Agree?	Why?	Impact to child
I will often talk to teachers for my children.			
I will often advocate for my children instead of letting them do it themselves.			
People tell me I am overly involved in my children's lives.			
People tell me that I am overprotective. But the world is a very scary place and I need to make sure my children are always safe.			

Once you are finished, reflect on your answers. Can you see ways in which your beliefs negatively impact your children? Are there beliefs you think should be changed?

_____

_____

_____

_____

_____

_____

_____

_____

_____

_____

_____

_____

_____

_____

_____

etc.), people with SAD consistently demonstrated impairments (Higa-McMillan & Ebesutani, 2011). Researchers disagree as to the causal relationship between social anxiety and social competence deficits. Did a deficit in social skills cause the SAD to develop, or did the social anxiety and the resultant withdrawal from social situations result in deficits in social compentence? And does it matter?

My work has led me to believe that decreased social competence factors into the initial development of SAD, and the resultant reduction of "social practice" perpetrates the underdevelopment of social competence and feeds the anxiety. The factors involved in social competence, social skills development, the development of strong prosocial skills, and the ability to navigate our complicated social world with reasonable success are skills that need to be developed in anyone struggling with social anxiety. Rather than focusing on why this is true, I think our time is best spent helping address these concerns in our youth, something I will tackle later in the book.

AUTISM, SOCIAL COMMUNICATION, AND ANXIETY

As we've discussed in the book already, SAD is a complex disorder that can mirror many of the symptoms of other disorders, including autism spectrum disorder (ASD) and social communication disorder (SCD). Both ASD and the newly defined SCD, a pragmatic disorder adopted in the newly revised DSM-5 (American Psychiatric Association, 2013a), involve poor social skill development and weak social interaction skills. All three disorders impact a person's social functioning, typically resulting in some form of withdrawal and apprehension. Does this mean that they are part of the same thing? Or are those with ASD or SCD typically also impacted by social anxiety? The answer is more complex than the question.

As discussed in Chapter 1, SAD is characterized by an intense fear of socializing with others due to fears of embarrassment and/or social humiliation. Part of the differential rule-out for SAD involves the capacity for the development of "typical" social skills and social competence. This definition alone points to SAD as a separate and unique disorder from ASD or SCD.

However, the answers don't end there. As I've also indicated earlier in this chapter, the causal relationship between social skill development and social competency and SAD is unclear, with some researchers hinting to the deficits in social competency as being a foundation for the development of SAD. In this case, one could assume that children with ASD and SCD would typically develop SAD. Again, this answer is also too simplistic.

The truth is that the overlap and comorbidity between these three conditions is significant. It is also, I would argue, less important than we might initially think.

Figure 1 shows a side-by-side comparison of SAD, ASD, and SCD. Clearly the three disorders are unique. Research has provided guidelines for differential diagnoses of these disorders, focusing on the child's ability to develop social skills at all, and the impact of the anxiety (children with SAD *and* SCD or ASD are more impacted by their anxiety than children with SAD alone (White & Schiry, 2011). This book is not about the differential diagnoses between these conditions, however. More important, I believe, is understanding how these similar diagnoses can interact and what parents can do to improve outcomes. For now, it is important to know that children diagnosed with ASD and/or SCD can and do sometimes present with SAD and it is an important consideration when developing strategies to support these children. In all three cases, children with these conditions often feel isolated and lonely, putting them at risk for depression (White & Schiry, 2011).

So how can parents help to support these complex cases? Researchers have consistently indicated that interventions that combine cognitive behavioral therapy techniques, something I discuss in length in later chapters, with parental involvement and the necessary language scaffolding for students with ASD of SCD (including the use of visual supports or less complex oral language) have the best outcomes (White et al., 2010; White, Ollendick, Scahill, Oswald, & Albano, 2009; White & Schiry, 2011). Tip Sheet #6 highlights specific strategies parents can adopt to help their child with ASD or SCD reduce his or her social anxiety, improve self-evaluation skills, and generalize skills into various settings. All of these strategies work best when combined with therapy that focuses on a cognitive behavioral approach.

SAD, ASD, and SCD

Attribute or Characteristic	Social Anxiety Disorder	Autism Spectrum Disorder	Social Communication Disorder
Avoidance	Avoidant of social situations for fear of embarrassment or humiliation	Often avoids due to disinterest and/or related to communication problems	Typically occurs related to difficulties with social communication and possible language delays
Anxiety/Fear	Primary motivation behind actions; lives in a state of significant fear and anxiety; will self-report anxiety and fear	Does not self-reflect and does not report periods of anxiety; if anxiety is apparent, it is notated by others first	Needs to be taught to recognize and label anxiety and other intense emotions; once taught, can self-identify anxiety and/or fear
Social Initiation	Avoids social initiation related to anxiety and the fear of negative evaluation	Often disinterested in initiations; needs to be taught how to initiate	Struggles to initiate despite a desire to do so; once taught, can initiate with others.
Friendships	Capable of developing reciprocal friendships, but seldom forms many related to fear and poor social skill development	Often disinterested in forming reciprocal friendships; if friendships are formed, they are typically with adults or younger peers; parallel play more typical; reciprocity difficult to develop	Needs assistance in developing reciprocal friendships due to pragmatic difficulties—this is particularly true as complexities of social communication increases with age; requires direct teaching of skills including teaching, modeling, role-playing, and generalizing

Figure 1. Differences between SAD, ASD, and SCD.

Figure 1. Continued.

Attribute or Characteristic	Social Anxiety Disorder	Autism Spectrum Disorder	Social Communication Disorder
Behavior Patterns	Typically internalizes stress/anxiety, resulting in periods of withdrawal and avoidance, as well as depression-like behaviors; will act out as a means to avoid or escape	Behaviors typically serve a communicative or sensory need; will act out as a means to communicate a protest or get/reject something; behaviors often happen to fill sensory needs as well	Externalizing behaviors often occur as a means of communication or related to increased frustration over a failure to communicate needs and wants socially
Communication	Capable of appropriate communication skills; however, will often avoid communication opportunities in larger groups or when anxiety is triggered	May be nonverbal or have limited verbal skills; typically has delays in social communication domains; requires learning a consistent and reliable way to communicate needs and wants	Delays in social communication; may also have expressive or receptive language delays; requires direct teaching/intervention to correct language problems

Tip Sheet #6

Interventions to Improve Anxiety Management in Children With ASD and SCD

Deficit Area	Intervention
Poor social skill development	• Identify missing social skills • Explicitly teach social skills • Use language scaffolding to support language deficits, including visual supports and reinforcement procedures • Consider the use of video modeling as appropriate to assist this process
Difficulties with self-evaluation	• Utilize social communication tools to help children identify *why* and *when* to use various social skills • Begin by having children explain why they behave a certain way; encourage them to look for environmental clues if they are unsure • Scaffold language demands as needs, using visual supports like graphic organizers
Difficulties with threat perception	• Combine with self-evaluation and social skill interventions • Ask child to look for evidence supporting his or her perceptions • Use graphic organizer or similar tool to begin discerning threats (real from perceived) • Use social stories to assist methods
Avoidance of social events	• Determine cause of avoidance • Scaffold supports to assist in reintroduction of avoided event • Start very small • Increase time in social setting gradually • Provide language supports to help child express distress • Make sure the above areas are addressed before adding too many previously avoided situations

Chalk Talk: The Case for Embedding Social Skills Curriculum

Most of us can agree that schools are microcosms of society, reflective of the social milieu we live in daily. There are expectations for students to initiate and reciprocate social interactions. We encourage and teach cooperative learning, the development of friendships, and the ability to solve minor conflicts. The goal is to develop successful members of society, not just academically, but socially. And yet, despite this lofty goal, we often fail to address and teach prosocial behaviors and social skills. Educators assume these skills are either learned at home or prior to the child's involvement at school. The result? The potential for school climates that allow bullying behaviors to develop and for children to be at increased risk for the development of social anxiety.

One of the best ways to counteract the potential for less-than-healthy school climates is to incorporate prosocial skill training within the global school climate. Integrating the concepts of responsibility and respect, motivation to learn, and a caring community serve to help the school community foster prosocial behaviors (Kidron & Fleischman, 2006). Focusing on positive behaviors and specifically teaching, rewarding, and highlighting behaviors that include basic social skill development (i.e., listening, following rules, asking for help, etc.) also help create a school climate focused on the development of prosocial behavior.

Although a schoolwide approach is a great foundation for a positive school climate, most teachers can only directly influence what happens in their classrooms. Tip Sheet #7 provides many examples of the types of curriculum that can serve to educate students academically and support the development of prosocial skills. Take a look at the list and alter it to fit the unique needs of your classroom. In addition to enhancing the culture of caring within your class, these activities will support positive behaviors in your students and help more anxious students find comfort within your room, resulting in improved student outcomes.

Tip Sheet #7

Activities That Foster Prosocial Skills

The following list of classroom activities will foster the development of prosocial skills and increase student safety and achievement:

- Use open-ended activities to promote creative play with peers.
- Encourage both verbal discussion and problem solving.
- Include a variety of books/stories related to perspective taking, diversity, and feelings.
- Use team-building creativity exercises throughout the school year, not just to "break the ice" at the beginning of the year.
- Directly teach prosocial behaviors and expectations.
- Model prosocial behavior and social competency.
- Use choice and consequences within the classroom environment consistently.

MEET DREW

Drew is a senior at a comprehensive high school. We met during his sixth-grade year when his parents scheduled an appointment to discuss their concerns. At the time of our meeting, Drew had been diagnosed with Asperger's syndrome, social anxiety (then called social phobia), and a potential mood disorder. In addition to the medical management of many of his symptoms, Drew received ongoing private therapy in the areas of speech and language pathology, social skills development, and more traditional psychotherapy to address his mood and anxiety-related issues. Drew's parents contacted me due to increasing concerns regarding school avoidance, peer interactions, and his propensity for seeking out students who struggled with their own behavioral control. Drew had struggled with his behavior in his previous school.

DREW'S STORY

Drew wandered into my office during the second week of sixth grade. Standing taller than most of his classmates, he had a reserved nature I immediately attributed to his autism spectrum disorder diagnosis. He sat and looked around my office, making a few comments about the various comic-inspired pictures, knick-knacks, and calendar I had. I asked him why his parents wanted him to visit me and his answer surprised me with its insight—"I struggle with people. And not just because of the Asperger's. I struggle because I just know they're going to humiliate me. So I'd rather not come to school at all."

I knew at this moment that we would be able to find some sort of common ground to begin the work of walking through his fears and anxiety. Over the next several weeks, Drew shared his earliest memories of school and being anxious about social context. He stated that his first experiences in kindergarten and first grade were negative. He wasn't able to tolerate the sensory overload that came with public school—the noise in the hallways and in class, the smells during lunch, the visual appearance of clutter in his classroom. It was so overwhelming, he said, that he felt he needed to hide himself away from it all.

So he did. His parents reported that Drew would often climb under his desk, close his eyes, cover his ears, and rock while singing. This behavior is what eventually led to his diagnosis, they stated.

But it wasn't just this behavior that eventually led to Drew's feelings at school. His peers did not react adversely to his rocking or crying. They didn't snicker when he hid under his chair. In fact, they were very accepting—until later in his elementary career.

Drew had attended several social skills classes for a few years. These classes gave him a lot of basic socialization skills that resulted in a significant reduction of the behaviors highlighted earlier. He no longer reacted adversely to the sensory overload of school. He did not hide or sing or rock at inappropriate times. By fourth grade, he appeared to behave much like his classmates. In fact, according to Drew's parents, his classmates didn't think of him as anything other than a typical peer.

One day, he had to present a project in front of the class. Drew was at a new school and this was the first presentation he had to make in front of his new friends. He practiced his speech over and over in the mirror at home. He rehearsed with his parents and was completely prepared when the day of his presentation arrived.

Unfortunately, life doesn't always go as planned. On the day of Drew's scheduled presentation, there was a substitute teacher. She was unaware of Drew's need for order. So, when she told Drew there would be no time for his presentation, she did not know she was disrupting his entire perception of the world. Drew reacted badly. He yelled, screamed, and had a tantrum. His peers watched, shocked. Drew ran from the room and wound up in a long conversation with the principal before going home with his parents.

The next day, Drew's regular teacher had returned. Although aware of Drew's difficulties the day before, she was not aware of what triggered the outburst, other than the idea that Drew really wanted to do his presentation. So, she asked Drew to come to the front of the class and give his presentation first thing. It wasn't on the schedule, nor was it what Drew expected. He walked up to the front of the class and opened his mouth to speak. But fear choked back his words. His hands began to shake and he promptly forgot everything he was going to say. Drew ran from the room, but not before a few classmates snickered and laughed.

From that day forward, according to Drew, his life changed. He resisted going to school, resisted any form of group work or presentations and struggled with his anger control. His parents increased his social skills classes and therapy. The increased support helped a little, but Drew continued to struggle through fourth and fifth grade.

Drew and I worked on understanding what happened that day, including how to reduce his anticipatory anxiety and increase his flexible thinking. Most importantly, I wanted to tap into his evident self-awareness and increase both Drew's awareness and discernment.

Self-regulation is difficult in children with behaviors consistent with ASD. It was definitely difficult with Drew. Over the course of 3 years, we were able to make marginal gains in his self-awareness and discernment, but much of the self-reflection occurred after the fact, using tools like the one in Worksheet #6. Unless we could engage that awareness during or precipitating events, I was not confident that we'd be able to make long-term strides in Drew's social anxiety at school.

His private therapist and I stayed in contact throughout Drew's middle school experience, hoping to support each other's area of work. Drew did reduce his absenteeism and behavioral outbursts at school.

High school was a different story. Drew struggled with the initial transition, resorting back to his anxious and externalizing behaviors. He resisted attending school and when he did attend, he resisted engaging in class, especially with any performance-based tasks. He required more support at school, including additional school-based counseling.

By his second year of school, he received counseling in an individual setting. The counselor reported great progress within that setting. Unfortunately, the progress did not translate into progress within the typical classroom. Drew continued to struggle with his behavior when frustrated and continued to

Worksheet #6
What Did I Do?

Directions: Think about the event(s) that triggered your behavior. Complete this worksheet indicating the event, what emotion you felt (use your emotional vocabulary if needed), and the intensity of your emotions. Combine this tool with Worksheet #11: Understanding My Triggers (p. 107) to create action plans and change your responses.

How Upset Am I Now? 1–5 scale: 1 = not upset; 5 = extremely upset

Event and Behavior	Emotion	How Upset Am I Now?
Example: *I was called on in class and started to cry*	*Scared, distrusting*	*3*

avoid performance-based tasks and socially charged activities (e.g., school dances, lunch in the main quad, etc.).

Drew has plans to attend a junior college and live at home once he finishes high school. He continues to struggle with anxiety in social venues. Whether this anxiety is more related to his diagnosis of ASD or SAD is unknown. What is clear is that Drew identified his anxiety as connected to his perception about his peers and his avoidance of humiliation and embarrassment, a definition that points to behaviors consistent with SAD.

LESSONS LEARNED

Drew's story illustrates several key points. First, it relates to the obvious social barriers encountered by children diagnosed with ASD or social communication problems. Drew's initial ability to connect and interact socially was compromised at a young age, requiring significant intervention and support. However, the support and social skills training was not enough to eliminate Drew's anxiety. His difficulties generalizing the new skills into the social venue of school further hampered his social development, in addition to the rigid thinking common with ASD.

Does this mean all children with ASD or similar disorders are destined to exhibit behaviors that mirror social anxiety? Not necessarily. But it does indicate that school professionals, as well as parents, should be prepared to support and assist children in this area. The more complications the student faces when attempting to both develop social competency and practice new social skills, the more likely the child will link social events to the emotions associated with anxiety. It is this link, in my opinion, that sets the stage for potentially pervasive social anxiety symptoms.

Drew's case also illustrates the complexities of children, social skill development, performance, and expectations. Every moment in a child's life is a teachable moment, an opportunity to reinforce specific skills that can counteract anxiety-inducing tasks. Take a look at Worksheet #7 and consider some of the ways to incorporate social skills competency training into everyday life. Utilizing every teachable moment makes the acquisition of social competency organic and "normal," even for children who struggle in this area.

Worksheet #7

My Teachable Moments

Directions: Think about the various typical activities you engage in with your child. Complete the chart with those activities, thinking about the social skills and competencies that are practiced within that activity. Then take a moment to think of additional opportunities to practice these skills.

Everyday Activity	Social Skills/Social Competency	Additional Opportunities for Practice
Example: Getting ready for school	• Setting goals • Breaking down tasks • Setting priorities • Delaying gratification • Following directions • Frustration tolerance • Calming yourself	• Getting ready for a party • Unexpected change in plans • Getting ready to leave the house

Concluding Thoughts

This chapter has focused on the environmental aspects of SAD, exploring everything from parenting styles to fear conditioning to cognitive bias. By now, you clearly see how complex the development of social anxiety is and why it can be a difficult beast to slay.

Despite the complexities of the disorder, I hope that you are also beginning to see the potential for positive interventions. Understanding the impact of parenting styles can give you the motivation to change or improve your approaches to parenting within your household. Reflecting on fear conditioning can point to the types of supports your child may need to help recondition his or her reactions to fear. Understanding cognitive biases and knowing the ways in which you and your children are impacted can help you develop strategies to retrain the brain. More than anything, I hope the chapter has led you to something I know from my own work in this area—while SAD is pervasive and difficult, it is not hopeless. Understanding the complexities of everything that supports the development and maintenance of social anxiety is the first step to decreasing the impact of the disorder on daily functioning.

The next chapter illustrates the many ways social anxiety impacts those suffering with it, and shows a few more ways we can understand and address SAD.

CHAPTER 4

The Impact of
Social Anxiety

"I have missed out on professional and social opportunities as a result of my social anxiety in anticipation of the scenario. While some people may assume social anxiety only happens to introverts, it happens to extroverts as well. It is dependent on the context whether my social anxiety is triggered or not. Many times friends and families have criticized my apprehension to participate in an activity based on my ability to participate in another. They don't understand that all social situations are NOT the same. With this being said, it only adds a secondary layer to my anxiety. As if feeling anxious isn't bad enough, now I have others feeding into my tendency to beat myself up because I don't understand why I am this way any better than they do . . . I just know it to be true!

I have worked with children with social anxiety. While some have been able to articulate, others are too young to use their words to do so . . . but the behavior speaks quite eloquently. No artificial consequence has the capacity to override the powerful influence of the social anxiety. It is not enjoyable. It is not volitional. They are not 'getting something out of it.' Often these individuals have been inaccurately labeled as a 'behavior problem,' 'noncompliant,' or 'disobedient.'

I have witnessed social anxiety impact families and children both in and out of school settings. When someone in the group, student, peer, parent, child, sibling, etc., suffers from social anxiety, it impacts everyone. It can manifest in a variety of ways. Someone is being left behind, often with an additional consequence for 'not behaving.' Someone/all have to stay back because either the individual cannot stay alone or someone is not available to stay with them, which can cause a variety of negative reactions in all parties involved. Sometimes, an individual is forced to enter an anxiety-producing situation. Then I have seen them chastised for their behavior often accompanied by a variety of threats and/or unpleasant consequences. The anxious individual does not enjoy the experience. The other parties do not enjoy the experience. In the end, the anxious individual is blamed." —Cathy, an adult with SAD who works as a behaviorist within the school setting

The previous three chapters examined the biological and behavioral precursors and triggers that can lead to the development of social anxiety disorder. This chapter focuses on the impact this diagnosis can have on overall functioning, the factors that can maintain the disorder, and ways to interrupt the disruptive nature of social anxiety.

SAD does not develop because of a single trait, genetic link, harsh word, or embarrassing situation. It is complex, multidimensional, and involves both nurture and nature, as this chapter will highlight.

Behavior Inhibition Revisited

Behavior inhibition (BI), as we learned in Chapter 2, is a significant precursor of the development of SAD (Schwartz, Snidman, & Kagan, 1999). Children who exhibit BI experience heightened levels of threat awareness, leading to increased anxiety and distress when faced with unfamiliar social environments. This often results in withdrawal from these environments. The pattern of threat detection, heightened fear responses, and withdrawal can become a cycle that leads to SAD. Once developed, the treatment for social anxiety can be difficult. This is especially true if the pattern of behaviors leading to the diagnoses happens at a very young age (Mesa et al., 2011). Understanding how to respond to a child with an inhibited temperament in a way that disrupts the cycle from habituating will help shield the child against the development of SAD.

Although the research around BI is somewhat scarce, much of it suggests that behavior inhibition is stable throughout the lifespan in a specific subset of children. This means that without some form of direct intervention, a child who exhibits significant fear in new social situations and withdraws will continue to demonstrate similar behaviors throughout his or her lifetime (Fox, Henderson, Marshall, Nichols, & Ghera, 2005). However, the research also speculates that when that same child receives direct interventions through parenting style or other means, the BI will become less stable (Rapee, 2014). This is great news for the parent worried that his or her child with an inhibited temperament will develop SAD.

What are the specific interventions that help reduce the stability of BI in children? From my experience, teaching children how to navigate social venues at an early age, as well as providing ample opportunities to successfully participate in social events, will help build confidence within those scenarios. This confidence undermines the inhibition. The result is improved outcomes and at least some reduction in the likelihood that SAD will develop.

Tip Sheet #8 includes additional ways in which building a child's social confidence can help reduce the negative impact of behavior inhibition on children. The take-home message here is the importance of allowing children to gain confidence within their environment by letting them do the things they are capable of doing. Guidance is great, but doing too much for our children can result in more than a dependent child. We could inadvertently set the stage for the future development of SAD.

Perfectionism and Performance

For some students, SAD is related to the potential for humiliation in the classroom. The child is afraid that he or she will make a mistake in class, be corrected by the teacher in some way, and be teased by his or her classmates. This fear translates to a threat within the anxious child, resulting in distress. Gifted children and those who wrestle with perfectionism can be even more impacted in this scenario.

Perfectionism is often thought of as a bad thing, a behavior or trait born out of anxiety that ultimately inhibits a child from doing their best. However, I prefer Silverman's perspective that perfectionism itself is neutral. It is a trait that can either be harnessed into a tool that drives our commitment to excellence, or become the yoke around our neck that

Tip Sheet #8

Building Confidence

Intervention	Why It Helps
Give the child a job (at home and/or at school)	• Connects the child to the home/school environment • Provides opportunities for light social connection • Provides opportunities for success
Performance-based praise	• Reinforces positive behaviors • Links praise to specific performance-based tasks, giving meaning and validity to the praise
Teach social skills and social competencies	• Helps the child develop needed skill bank • Gives the child a sense of potential mastery and self-efficacy
Create a culture of caring at home and at school	• Communicates safety • Reduces a child's fears • Minimizes opportunities for negative social interactions • Supports the development of prosocial skills
Teach problem-solving skills (including creative problem solving skills)	• Encourages creativity in all children • Builds esteem and self-efficacy • Increases resiliency

stifles our ability to complete even the most simple of tasks (Silverman, 2007).

In my own practice, I find Hébert's (2011) idea of perfectionism as an extension of our cultural pursuit of excellence accurate. Most of us would never question the artist, athlete, or entrepreneur who works tirelessly to perfect his or her craft. Yet we question the intent of the perfectionist child, the one who is up until the wee hours studying for a test (Hébert, 2011).

Often it isn't the perfectionism that causes most parents to grow concerned. It is the anxious behavior that is so often present in the perfectionist child that makes parents worry. In my experience, however, the anxiety isn't coming from the commitment to high standards that perfectionism represents. Anxiety and resultant performance inhibition often comes from the mismatch between the child's desire to perform well, and the perception that anything other than *perfect* equates to complete failure. In these children, mistakes are not viewed as opportunities to learn and grow, but proof that they are somehow flawed.

This is even more problematic in the child who is also afraid that his or her perceived imperfections will make him or her vulnerable to humiliation from peers. In these cases, the perfectionism quickly takes on a life of its own as the child becomes crippled by his or her need to avoid mistakes for fear of embarrassment. It is easy to see how quickly a case of social anxiety could develop in this situation.

It is important that both parents and educators guard against adversely contributing to the negative aspects of perfectionism by either setting unrealistic expectations or focusing on product over learning. This is not to say that high expectations should be avoided. On the contrary, I think high expectations are appropriate. But parents and educators need to take a balanced approach when working with the perfectionist child, teaching him or her that mistakes are part of the learning process and indicative that he or she is being stretched outside of his or her comfort zone.

Worksheet #8 can help guide you as you find the balance between pushing your child toward growth and feeding the negative aspects of his or her perfectionism. Use this guide anytime you begin to suspect that you are going too far with your child.

Selective Mutism, School Refusal, and Other Extremes

Social anxiety is difficult to manage in most situations. This difficulty becomes even stronger when it morphs into something more extreme. Selective mutism is one example of the significant extremes of an anxiety disorder.

Selective mutism is defined as a childhood anxiety disorder characterized by a child's inability to talk or effectively communicate at school or in unfamiliar settings despite being able to communicate in an age-ap-

Worksheet #8

Am I Going Too Far?

Directions: Complete the worksheet below, paying close attention to your child's responses.

Request	Goal	Child's Response	Was the Goal Achieved?
Example: I told my child to study harder for her test due to poor grades on her last test.	• Instill desire to improve grades • Instill high expectations	Student cried and then started to study. She worked for 2 hours on the material.	She made careless errors on her test and got another poor grade.

Review the worksheet. Do you notice any trends? Are there any changes you'd like to make to your approach?

_____

_____

_____

_____

_____

_____

_____

_____

_____

propriate manner in the home and/or familiar settings (Shipon-Blum, n.d.). Most cases of selective mutism can be traced back to social anxiety, as the apparent mutism typically arises out of an intense fear of being humiliated or embarrassed at school or in unfamiliar settings. Many parents will confuse the behavior of a child with selective mutism as being excessively shy. However, like most cases of shyness, selective mutism isn't about behavioral avoidance. And it isn't as readily managed as most cases of shyness. Selective mutism requires significant interventions similar to many of the interventions outlined for use with SAD throughout the book.

It is important to note that children with selective mutism will demonstrate it in a variety of ways, ranging from being completely mute with teachers and peers, to being able to whisper to one or two people only. Some children may even become oppositional in response to parents and teachers forcing them to speak instead of understanding the anxious aspects of the disorder. For those children, the mutism can persist and become highly habituated, similar to many of the avoidant and inhibition behaviors associated with social anxiety. The key to helping a child with selective mutism is to focus on building confidence and helping the child correct his or her errors in cognition.

Selective mutism isn't the only extreme potential outcome for SAD. School refusal, in some cases, has also been shown to be correlated to to social anxiety (Kearney, Gauger, Schafer, & Day, 2011). Here, the oppositional behavior associated with children who refuse to attend school or who are chronically tardy is an outward expression of the significant social anxiety related to fears of adverse social connections at school.

Like children with selective mutism, it would be easy to assume the school refusal is something other than an anxiety problem. In truth, there are many reasons why children refuse to attend school, and sometimes fear of negative social interactions is the key. These children resist being called on in class, refuse to read aloud, and avoid partipating in class. After years of struggling with their fear, they eventually stop coming to school all together, claiming to be sick or just refusing to attend.

Understanding the true reasons for school refusal is the first step to understanding the role of SAD, if any. When social anxiety is part of the cause, it is important to focus on mitigating the child's fear, correcting the faulty thinking, and helping the child return to school for opportunities to work through the anxiety as soon as possible.

I've covered a few of the more significant extremes associated with SAD. Additional comorbid conditions including depression, seperation anxiety, and generalized anxiety disorder are also found alongside social anxiety. Research indicates that social anxiety predates many of these conditions, although the connections between the disorders are not widely understood at this time (Mesa et al., 2011). Regardless, outcomes for SAD are lowered when a comorbid condition is present, pointing again to the need for intervention and support as early as possible to ensure positive outcomes.

More Than Being Oppositional

Most parents and educators do not consider oppositional behavior to be symptomatic of social anxiety. After all, children with SAD tend to withdraw. They isolate and internalize their stress. Oppositional behavior, on the other hand, refers to defiant, noncompliant, tantrum-like behavior. These behaviors are considered externalizing, the opposite of what is expected with social anxiety. So how can they be related?

Researchers have found a connection between anxiety and externalized behavior throughout history (Kearney et al., 2011). Current researchers continue to support the link between SAD and oppositional behavior, indicating that tantruming, defiance in class, and escape behaviors can be connected to the child's fear of social humiliation. In my own practice, I have found several cases in which a student will escape a class or tantrum to get out of having to participate in a lesson. When a functional analysis of the behavior is conducted, it often becomes clear that the student not only feared the event he or she was escaping, but the child lacked the necessary social compentecies to express his or her fear and seek help.

I will go into great detail how parents can begin to analyze their child's behavior. For now, I'd like you to use Worksheet #9 to begin to isolate the specific ways SAD is impacting your child, both in terms of internalized behaviors (withdrawal, avoidance) and externalized behav-

Worksheet #9

Understanding My Child's Behaviors

Directions: Complete the worksheet with your child to determine the internal and external behaviors associated with each event.

Trigger	Child's Response	Internal or External Behavior
Example: My child had a math test.	During the test she reported that her mind went blank. When she came home, she was on edge and explosive.	• Internal—mind went blank • External—explosive behaviors

Review the responses on the worksheet. What do you notice about your child's behaviors?

_____

_____

_____

_____

_____

iors (tantrums, defiance). Understanding the ways in which your child exhibts his or her anxiety, as well as the triggers, will assist you as you develop interventions to improve the outcome for your child.

When Social Anxiety Morphs Into Something More

Chapter 1 highlighted some of the conditions that mirror social anxiety, often causing difficulties with diagnosis. In addition to possible misdiagnoses, research does indicate several conditions that are comorbid with social anxiety. As discussed earlier, externalized behavior often occurs with SAD (Beidel & Turner, 2007). When this behavior becomes extreme, it will often be diagnosed as oppositional defiance disorder (ODD), or even conduct disorder (CD). These behavior disorders are characterized by noncompliance, defiance, and tantrum behavior. In their more extreme forms, they include breaking school rules, high-risk behaviors, school refusal, and more extreme antisocial behavior. In the case of a child with SAD, the function of the behavior is to escape the source of his or her anxiety or fear, namely, social humiliation.

Social anxiety will typically predate the appearance of the externalized behavior. However, it will often not be identified until the behaviors become extreme and disruptive. Therefore, the behavior disorder may be diagnosed first. It is important in all cases of externalized behaviors to look at the communicative function of the behavior for both intervention development and to understand the source of the problem and support the child proactively. I will explain how to begin to determine the function of behavior in Chapter 9. For now, it is only important to understand that social anxiety can lead to behavioral challenges and that SAD can exist comorbidly with ODD.

Similar to behavioral disorders, sometimes attention problems (ADHD) are diagnosed in addition to SAD (Beidel & Turner, 2007). Most of the time, this is not a comorbid condition as much as it is a misdiagnosis. Children with anxiety will often appear inattentive and impulsive as they try to avoid the perceived source of their anxiety. Again, keeping track of your child's behavior, as well as the potential function,

Tip Sheet #9

Keeping a Behavior Journal

- Decide on which behavior(s) to target.
- Write down each behavioral occurrence, including what happened immediately before and what happened immediately after.
- Keep brief anecdotal notes regarding the strategies used and/or any changes in routine, medications, etc.
- Keep a daily log at first, with a goal of keeping the log as needed once the behaviors are under control.

can help skilled professionals begin to make a differential diagnosis. The more information you can provide to those working with your child, the more accurate the diagnosis and treatment. Tip Sheet #9 can help you begin to keep a simple behavior journal about your child. I will delve into this more in Chapters 8 and 9, but starting a journal today is a great first step.

Perhaps the most common comorbid diagnoses with SAD are generalized anxiety disorder (GAD) and depression (Beidel & Turner, 2007; Starr, Davila, La Greca, & Landoll, 2011). GAD is often diagnosed in cases where the SAD is linked to hereditary or specific neurobiological roots. The fear circuitry is hardwired for activation, and the child experiences anxiety related to not only the social milleu and fear of social failure, but in relation to most activities within the day. This level of anxiety requires significant interventions in order to correct the faulty thinking and reduce the negative impact of the anxious reaction. Utilizing skilled professionals, as well as enlisting help from the school is typically the best way to support the child.

Depression is the most prevalent comorbid condition, affecting as many as 34% of the those diagnosed with SAD (Kessler, Stang, Wittchen, Stein, & Walters, 1999). The relevance of this cannot be understated. People with comorbid SAD and depression report more significant symptoms, including increased episodes of depression and suicidality. In children, increased conflicts with friends and family and increased resistence to treatment is evident throughout the research (Starr et al., 2011). Given this information, it is crucial that parents seek assistance and support for their children when they suspect depression.

As with the other comorbid conditions referenced in the chapter, SAD typically precedes depression. The causal connection for this is unclear, but there can be no doubt that early recognition of SAD and early treatment is essential to mitigating the possible negative impact of both SAD and depression. Section III focuses on ways for families to reach out and get help when their children are showing signs of SAD.

One of the key considerations in supporting the child with both SAD and depression is understanding how the features of each disorder overlap, and utilizing inventions that address both. Table 1 highlights the overlapping cognitive, temperament, and interpersonal features of both SAD and depression, as well as interventions that may help. This table can help you know what aspects of your child's difficulties to focus on and which to address later. Again, early support and the assistance of a skilled professional is needed to help manage the negative aspects of this comorbidity.

The bottom line is this: If you suspect your child may struggle with both SAD and depression, seek help from a skilled professional as early as you can.

MORE THAN STUTTERING

Some of the most underresearched and misunderstood predisposing factors for the development of SAD are speech and language disorders. Speech-language pathologists often report that children with speech and language development problems demonstrate a host of externalizing and anxiety-like behaviors related to their specific language and/or speech impairment (SLI). Indeed, research regarding the impact of speech and language impairment on social skill development and behavior consistently points to a connection between the child's ability to communicate effectively and social behavior (Fujiki, Brinton, Isaacson, & Summers, 2001). These behaviors include avoidance of social interaction and withdrawal from peers.

Sounds a lot like social anxiety, doesn't it? In fact, the behavioral overlay between speech and language problems and the development of social

Table 1. SAD and Depression

Common Factors of SAD and Depression	Intervention
Rumination (Repetitive thinking of negative acts/events, especially postevent)	» Teach children how to recognize rumination » With young children, use distraction as a way to break negative cyclic thinking » Encourage use of gratitude journals » Teach discernment and mindfulness
Low optimism	» Use a gratitude journal » Practice shift perspective—retell negative events from a new POV to emphasize the positive » Create action plans with your child to improve on perceived areas of deficit » Build confidence through performance-based praise
Poor peer interactions and self-reported peer rejection	» Teach and practice social skills and social competency » Find like-minded peers
Peer victimizations	» Teach children what appropriate friendships look like » Teach children how to report acts of victimization » Teach children how to self-advocate » Utilize mental health assistance as needed

anxiety are significant. Children with SLI demonstrate weak social comptency, poor prosocial development, weak peer interaction skills (Conti-Ramsden & Botting, 2004), and a greater likelihood of avoidant behavior similar to that found with SAD.

Before I get too much further into social anxiety in the child with SLI, I think it is important to define a speech and language impairment. SLI is a communication disorder that can involve speech development (i.e., articulation or stuttering problems) and/or language development (i.e., delays in expressive or receptive language). Often a child will have a mismatch between expressive and receptive language, meaning he or she can understand more language than he or she can express. Sometimes the expressive language problems are related to oral motor problems, sometimes to development, and sometimes due to neurological processing. Children with deficits in their ability to communicate may act out due to frustration. They may also begin to withdraw from others due to their communication deficits.

In more severe cases, prolonged expressive language problems that haven't been addressed adequately can result in the development of symptoms related to social anxiety as children withdraw from others and begin to develop delays in their social competencies, increasing their apprehension within social situations (St. Clair, Pickles, Durkin, & Conti-Ramsden, 2011). Like many other cases we've discussed, a pervasive cycle of avoidance and increased skill deficits occurs. Although the anxiety often present at this point may not be formally diagnosed as SAD, many characteristics are present.

Table 2 highlights the behaviors that can result from a variety of situations involving children with SLI. Looking at this, it is easy to see how social anxiety can develop. The key is addressing the underlying problem of the SLI in addition to providing direct instruction on the missing social deficits and addressing any faulty thinking that may have become entrenched. These are complicated cases, typically. The more skilled professionals that can be involved in assisting the child with SLI and anxiety, the better.

Chalk Talk: When Students Struggle to Communicate

One of the most common concerns raised to me by educators involves students who struggle to communicate their ideas and the resultant impact, both in terms of student engagement and behavior. It is no secret that the student who is unable to communicate effectively struggles in terms of academics as well as social development. What is not always understood is the correlation between communication difficulties and behavioral control, including both externalized behaviors, like aggression and tantrums, and internalized behaviors, like avoidance and withdrawal. Further, many educators don't understand the connection between communication difficulties and social anxiety.

Deficits in communication areas can take many forms. For some students, poor oral motor control and planning result in articulation errors and dysfluency, or stuttering. Many of these students exhibit behaviors

Table 2. Communication Problems and Behavior

Behavior	Expressive Language Deficit	Receptive Language Deficit	Social Communication Disorder
Internalized behavior (withdrawal, avoidance, depression, anxiety)	**Why it happens:** Difficulty expressing needs and wants **What to do:** Address language development; provide alternative ways to communicate needs and wants; address specific anxiety concerns as needed	**Why it happens:** Difficulty understanding others' requests **What to do:** Address language development; provide alternative ways for the child to understand what is being communicated and what is expected; address specific anxiety concerns as needed	**Why it happens:** Difficulty understanding the social nuances of language **What to do:** Address language development; explicitly teach social communication skills; address withdrawal/avoidance behavior before it becomes habituated
Externalized behaviors (oppositional, explosive, breaking rules)	**Why it happens:** As a means of communicating needs and wants and/or due to increased frustration **What to do:** Address language development; provide alternative ways to communicate needs and wants; address behavior through positive behavior supports	**Why it happens:** Increased frustration related to communication problems **What to do:** Address language development; scaffold language needs using visual supports; address behaviors through positive behavior supports	**Why it happens:** Emotional overload due to increased communication expectations and reduced frustration tolerance **What to do:** Address social language development; scaffold language; script social responses as needed; practice new skills often; address behavior through positive behavior supports

consistent with social anxiety resulting from their struggles with oral communication. They may avoid situations in which they have to talk, avoid peer interactions, or withdraw from social communication in order to prevent potential ridicule related to their speech impairments. The cycle repeats, creating a lack of opportunity and practice of social skills and eventually a skill deficit—all related to initial difficulties with speech. Soon a pattern of social anxiety kicks in, and where there was one significant area of concern, there are now two. These students may not have been diagnosed with SAD, but their actions mirror cases of SAD completely.

Speech problems aren't the only communication domain that can lead to similar behaviors. Deficits in receptive and expressive language can also result in social behavioral problems (Hart, Fujiki, Brinton, & Hart, 2004). Students who struggle with being able to understand and use language are at a loss in a classroom. They are often unable to communicate with the teacher or their peers in ways that are as sophisticated as their typically developing classmates. They will often miss the subtleties of language, including intent and innuendo. When this happens, many of these students will resort to less sophisticated ways to get their message across—tantruming and/or aggressive behaviors. Additionally, these students may withdraw from the educational experience all together, avoiding interactions with peers or classroom experiences. When this happens, the same cycle of avoidance-deficit growth-avoidance occurs, setting the stage for additional anxiety-related conditions to develop, including social anxiety.

The key to preventing some of the negative outcomes is to address the underlying problem of the communication deficits. Additional interventions will be needed to support the student who is also exhibiting social anxiety or oppositional behaviors. The list of strategies in Tip Sheet #10 is provided as a reference point for educational teams to begin to address the complexitites of students with communication deficits and comorbid social behavioral concerns. Use this list with educational teams (like the ones dicussed in Chapter 8) when working to support these students.

Tip Sheet #10

Tips for Helping With SAD and SLI

- Focus on teaching social skills and social communication first.
- Develop a common language for addressing behavioral concerns and anxiety.
- Utilize visual supports and other language scaffolding techniques.
- Look for the communicative intent of behavior and address that first.
- Make sure the environment is caring and supportive.
- After the student develops an emotional vocabulary and a foundation for social communication skills, focus on emotional coaching to address social anxiety.

MEET SONG

Song's parents and I met through one of my parenting workshops when Song was in third grade. Although Song was a strong student and seldom demonstrated any behavioral difficulties at school or at home, her parents were concerned with her unwillingness to talk at school. They stated that her teachers over the past 2 years were alarmed over her complete lack of speech during the school day, despite numerous interventions. Song was referred to the school's speech-language pathologist the week of the parenting class. Her parents were confused over the referral, as they did not see any of the reluctance within the home setting. When asked to describe their daughter's communication habits outside of school, Song's parents indicated that Song was very "shy" and often refused to interact with others until she was comfortable with them.

Song's behavior was consistent with selective mutism, a condition described as an extreme version of social anxiety that impacts a child's ability to speak and communicate within a school setting for fear of humiliation and embarrassment. Song's parents needed information and practical strategies to help their daughter ease the stress she encountered within the school setting. I provided initial coaching to the family and helped them connect with community resources that could help them work through Song's mutism before it became habitual.

SONG'S STORY

Song's earliest memories of school are typical—the first day of preschool, shopping for school supplies with her mom after the first day of kindergarten, meeting new friends. As a first-generation American student, Song blended into the myriad students in her suburban school well. She was quiet and never disrupted the lessons, answered questions on her tests correctly, and was often observed quietly interacting with one or two students at lunch.

Kindergarten and first grade progressed with no significant concerns. She met her benchmarks for academic progress, exceeding them in math and science. When Song wasn't at school, she was taking enrichment classes for math, mastering the piano, or learning to play golf. There was no time for idle play in her household. Every activity was designed to strengthen her chances at getting into college—even at her young age. "Potential like hers should not be wasted," her mother told me when we first met.

Song appeared to enjoy her busy life. She never complained about missing play dates or parties. She relished in the attention she received from her coaches and teachers. In general, she seemed happy.

Things began to change at the start of second grade. Song's naturally reserved demeanor became even more withdrawn. Although she had one or two friends, she seldom expressed her opinions to them, choosing instead to subjugate her wants for theirs. If they wanted to play tetherball, she did— even though she hated the game. If they wanted to play in the grass, she complied—even though she got a rash every time.

In the classroom, Song's quiet demeanor became more noticeable. She never raised her hand to join in the discussion, resisted open participation in group conversations, and was reluctant to demonstrate her work on whiteboard activities. By the end of the first quarter, her teacher was concerned and called a meeting with her parents. "Song is struggling to communicate in school," her teacher told them. "I think she needs a speech evaluation as soon as possible." Song's parents were at a loss; Song communicated fine at home and to her coaches. They expressed their gratitude for the teacher's concern and never gave the matter further consideration.

By the end of second grade, Song's withdrawal from school had increased. Her teacher continued to express concern about Song's lack of clear communication. Song's grades continued to indicate proficient performance, and she continued to do very well within the context of golf and music.

Third grade brought increased concern from the school. A Student Study Team (SST) was convened and the school again recommended assessments in the area of speech and language to determine the root cause of the unwillingness to speak at school. It was at this point that I was asked to work with Song.

Within the first few meetings, it was clear that Song's reserved demeanor factored into the concern. Song approached new situations with some reluctance, not unusual given her age and the nature of our interactions. Song did warm-up relatively quickly, however, and by the third time we had met, Song was able to clearly communicate her feelings and beliefs.

Song stated that her reticence to communicate at school directly related to a bad experience at the end of first grade. Song had participated in a group activity that culminated with an argument with her groupmates. They told her she "wasn't allowed" to do any of the presentation because she spoke too softly. Although the group did complete the project and present it to the class, Song felt humiliated. She told me what had transpired and that she had simply decided that she was not going to participate in anything like that project again. Period.

Song and I worked on her faulty and catastrophic thinking for the next few weeks. In addition to my sessions with Song, I met with her parents three times. We developed reasonable expectations for Song's performance and worked on strategies for social competence development and stress management. After a few weeks, I gave Song's parents continuing exercises focused on social competency. In addition, Song expressed an interest in theatre, so I connected her parents with children's performance groups within the community.

Song reconnected to school within a year. She continued to excel and although she never became comfortable with group projects or public speaking, she did learn a few strategies to employ when she was required to present topics in class.

LESSONS LEARNED

Song's story has a much better ending than most cases of selective mutism, even the mild ones. The key in this situation was timing. Once Song's parents understood that the problem their daughter was having at school was significant, they quickly sought assistance and were active participants in the recovery process. Furthermore, Song's performance anxiety was related to a specific event. Her stress had not significantly generalized outside the purview of similar events, making it easier to address in academic counseling/coaching sessions.

Another key to the successful resolution of Song's anxiety was her interest in theatre. The skills learned within the context of acting can be transferred easily to the school setting, as Tip Sheet #11 illustrates. Many of these improvisation strategies can be adapted to use with the socially anxious child.

It's important to note that many cases of selective mutism do not resolve as easily or quickly as Song's did. I have worked with some students who are eventually hospitalized due to severe cases of selective mutism and the anxiety experienced by the child when forced to speak within the context of school. In cases such as these, it is critical for parents to involve a network of professionals, including mental health professionals, speech and language pathologists (as appropriate), school personnel, and potentially a psychiatrist and/or medical doctor.

Concluding Thoughts

There are many factors that can maintain and worsen social anxiety. Entrenched patterns of responding to crises, real and perceived, can increase behavior inhibition and a child's threat response. As the anxiety levels increase, the cycle perpetuates, often with significant results. Selective mutism, school refusal, and increased behavior problems can all result from the perpetual cycle of social anxiety. Comorbid conditions like generalized anxiety disorder and specific phobias can develop, as well as depression.

That is, unless successful interventions take place.

Children and adolescents need the adults around them to take notice of their social anxiety and intervene. The next chapters focus on the specific impact of social anxiety on school performance, relationship building, and overall functioning. Although social anxiety can be devastating, there is hope. Many interventions have been proven to be highly effective, especially if the anxiety is caught early, prior to the habituating of the negative behaviors. As you become familiar with the etiology and the impact of SAD, you will be able to see the anxiety and support it earlier, with improved outcomes for all.

Tip Sheet #11

Fake It 'Til You Make It

There are many improvisation and acting techniques that can help a socially anxious child work through his or her anxiety, even when it feels impossible to do so. The short list below highlights a few of the more common improvisation best practices that can be adapted for use with socially anxious children.

- **Transparency:** Learn to be transparent and authentic. Rather than hide the depth of your fears due to shame or potential embarrassment, own them. Tell a trusted adult that you are afraid of failing, speaking, out, etc. In the sharing, you will connect and the fear will begin to dissipate.
- **Be specific:** When you are anxious and afraid, it is easy to think *everything* is scary. The truth, however, is different. Usually there is a specific cause or root to your fear. Find that, address that, and the anxiety will lessen.
- **Let go:** Typically, the only way to move through your anxiety is to let go of both the fear and your inhibitions. This will be hard at first. Pretend you are a character in a play to reduce your initial resistance. Once you take a leap of faith, the second leap is easier.
- **"Yes, and . . .":** When life throws a curveball, rather than resist the change, go with it. Accept the situation and move forward. You may be surprised what happens when you release your expectations and embrace life's natural flow.
- **Play to your strengths:** We all have strengths. Discover yours and develop them. Return to your strengths whenever you need a boost.

This is not to say that there is nothing to do once the anxiety takes hold. I am a firm believer that it is never too late to intervene. The important thing is to understand your child and his or her anxiety, then do something to help.

PART II

Feeling Safe Inside Your Skin

CHAPTER 5

Social Anxiety Comes to School

> *"The biggest challenge is with my 6-year-old who took a long time to stop crying every day before school. She pled [with me] not to go and her first months in school were epic and difficult. It took about 3 academic years to get past this. Her teachers would have to walk her around school because she wouldn't stop crying. She seemed scared of the other kids.*
>
> *Her difficulties have had a huge impact on me by creating an anxious situation every morning that I still have not overcome inside. I often say I have PTSD from all those mornings of crying and tantrums about not wanting to go to school. She doesn't do it anymore, but I still wake anxious for the day. It's something I have to overcome myself now."* —Gina, parent of a child with social anxiety

By now you may be wondering exactly how social anxiety fits into the world of school, peer interactions, and the family. The first section of *Raising the Shy Child* focused on the specific characteristics of social anxiety, along with the predisposing, predicting, and maintaining factors. This next section will discuss the implications of social anxiety in all of its environments—school, peers, and home—as well as provide a few more strategies for supporting our children with behaviors consistent with social anxiety.

As you've likely guessed, some of the biggest negative impacts of SAD occur at school. As a child with social anxiety is asked to face increasingly difficult and complex academic and social challenges within the school setting, he or she is often confronted on a near constant basis with his or her own anxieties, often with negative results. This chapter will examine some of the specific ways anxiety impacts functioning within the context of school, as well as the contributing factors of parent and teacher involvement.

What Is a Normal Level of Performance Pressure?

We live in a high-pressure world. Schools have become more and more competitive and the push to achieve continues to grow. All students feel a certain amount of pressure to perform and excel. This can be particularly true in families where college attendance is expected and achievement is valued over effort.

Surviving the pressure cooker called school can be challenging for most students. Periods of increased stress and emotional breakdown occur. Learning the basic tricks for managing these moments is important for every student. Tip Sheet #12 provides a quick reference guide for managing the daily pressures most children face in today's world. Utilizing a few of the strategies provided can keep the pressure manageable.

The strategies outlined above work for most children. Children with SAD, however, may become overwhelmed more quickly than typical peers and may require more support. As stated previously, socially anxious children are triggered by events in which they assume they will experience social humiliation. This can include performance opportunities in the classroom like speaking in front of the class or doing whiteboard activities in math. Both of these activities can elicit a highly anxious response from the child with SAD.

It is important to help children manage the daily pressures of school before it becomes overwhelming. Utilize the strategies listed earlier in the chapter. Additionally, review the social skills most commonly used at school discussed later in this chapter. The combination of social skills development and managing performance pressures can go a long way to mediate the impact of performance concerns when they trigger social anxiety.

Tip Sheet #12

Beating the Pressure Trap

Teach children these quick ways to combat the pressures of school and life:

- Focus on healthy living, including appropriate eating, relaxation, sleeping, and exercise routines.
- Spend time relaxing every day. Teach your children different ways to relax. What works for one child may not work for another.
- Pay attention to how you talk to yourself. Positive self-talk can help to reduce the impact of pressure and stress.
- Learn to be mindful and realistic in your point of view.
- If you find yourself particularly stressed over a specific event, mentally rehearse the event, focusing on successfully completing the activity.

Learning to recognize and release pressure takes some time. Doing something small in this area every day can turn you into a pressure-beating machine in no time.

Social Skills Needed at School

Schools are social microcosms. Various levels of social skills are needed just to navigate the increasingly complex social expectations our children face as they move from grade to grade. These skills can be difficult to learn, especially for socially anxious students who fall into a cycle of avoidance. For these students, learning the needed social skills is elusive as their pattern of avoidance and withdrawal negate opportunities to learn and practice needed skills. It is important that these children receive additional supports for the development of necessary social competencies, including the acquisition of various social skills.

There are many social skills needed within the school setting (see Figure 2). These skills are best characterized as basic skills (including listening, following directions, and ignoring distractions), interpersonal skills (including turn-taking and initiating a conversation), and problem-solving skills (including asking for permission and accepting consequences).

The following skills are both the basic skills essential for success and the basic social skills that should be mastered. You'll notice that many of these are the very skills we teach both at home and at school.

- » Listen.
- » Follow the rules or directions.
- » Ignore distractions.
- » Ask for help.
- » Take turns.
- » Respect boundaries.
- » Stay calm.
- » Accept responsibility for your actions.
- » Accept "no" for an answer.
- » Treat others as you would like to be treated.

Figure 2. Critical school social skills.

Mastering these skills can help the socially anxious child improve his or her involvement at school and reinforce inclusionary behavior.

Teaching social skills involves directly teaching the skill, providing time to practice the skill, generalizing the skill in multiple environments and giving immediate performance feedback. Parents can be involved in any part of this process. Many times, schools offer some sort of social skills training within the school curriculum, usually as part of a larger positive behavior program on campus. If your school is using a social skills program, find out what skills are being taught and how. This information can help you know how to support the acquisition of the skills within the home setting.

If your school is not actively teaching social skills, you can work with your child at home. Observe your child in a variety of situations. Does he know how to listen or to ask for help? Does she know what do to when she receives a correction? If not, take a moment to teach and practice the missing skills.

Tip Sheet #13 recaps the steps to teach any social skill. The process is the same for each identified skill. Taking the time to actively teach social skills can help address the needs of our socially anxious youth and minimize the impact of the disorder on daily functioning at school.

Tip Sheet #13
Teaching Social Skills

Teaching social skills can be done in a small group or classwide. Best practice includes both direct teaching of the skill and opportunities for children to practice the skills in multiple settings.

1. Determine what skill is to be taught. Teach one skill per session.
2. Discuss the specific skill, including when the skill should be used and the benefits of using the skill.
3. Use visual models (like a cue card) to explain the steps of the skill. Refer to the Tip Sheet #26: Social Skills Scripts (p. 158) for more ideas.
4. Demonstrate the skill.
5. Role-play for practice.
6. Provide performance feedback as the skill is practiced.
7. Revisit previously learned skills frequently.

The Social Dynamics of School

As mentioned at the start of the chapter, schools are complex social environments. Friendships, differing social rules in the classroom and on the playground, and performance expectations can make navigating the social milieu of school difficult, especially for the child with social anxiety.

There are many factors that can influence a child's ability to socially function at school. The acquisition of social skills is one factor. Another is the ability to make close friendships. As a child moves from middle childhood toward adolescence, the need for a network of friends becomes greater. This can pose problems to the socially anxious child.

As mentioned in the previous section of the book, the development of strong social circles is significantly impacted by SAD. Children with social anxiety struggle not only with the initial forming of friendships, but with the quality of the relationships as well. Research has indicated a tendency for socially anxious youth to form friendships with similarly shy and withdrawn children (Rubin, Wojslawowicz, Rose-Krasnor, Booth-LaForce, & Burgess, 2006). This, according to the researchers,

Tip Sheet #14

Building Social Competency

Several types of learned behaviors make up social competency. The following list includes the most important types of behaviors children need to learn in order to develop strong social competency.

- Teach children how to recognize and manage their own behavior and emotions. Using Tip Sheet #5: Building an Emotional Vocabulary (p. 40) can be helpful with this, as well as several of the other self-reflection tools.
- Teach children to accurately perceive social cues and responses. Use Worksheet #3: Threat Discernment (p. 30) and similar activities to assist with this.
- Teach perspective and consequences to children.
- Teach relaxation techniques. Using the social skills training model can help.
- Teach specific problem-solving skills.
- Use positive role models to help coach these behaviors in your children

can decrease the beneficial aspects of friendship by reducing support and skill develop and potentially increase the chances of peer victimization. Although I don't believe that such friendships should be discouraged, I do think it is important to focus on building social competencies within your child. Tip Sheet #14 includes specific ways to grow your child's social competencies and reduce the negative impact of social anxiety.

Another Look at School Refusal

As mentioned in Chapter 4, school refusal is one of the potential extreme results of social anxiety. School refusal seldom starts out as a full refusal to attend school. More typically, it starts with a child refusing specific tasks or classes. Over time, if the core issues affecting the child are not discovered and supported, missing an assignment or class turns into missing a day or two. Within a relatively short amount of time, the absences can morph into a significant case of school refusal.

It is important to address cases of task refusal, truancy, and absences early. This is especially true when working with a child with social anxiety. Utilize the previous suggestion of maintaining a behavior journal to help determine the cause of the refusal and avoidance. If the child is anticipating failure, then work to correct his or her faulty thinking. If the child does know how to ask for help, then teach the specific skill of asking for help or self-advocacy.

Worksheet #10 can help you identify the possible reasons and interventions for your child's avoidance. Use it as a guide to inform you of possible strategies to help break your child's cycle of avoidance before it becomes entrenched.

THE BULLY AND THE SOCIALLY ANXIOUS

Children with social anxiety are at increased risk for bullying. Many of the symptoms of the socially anxious are the exact characteristics looked for in a potential victim (Erath, Flanagan, & Bierman, 2007). Social avoidance, difficulties making friendships, and poor interpersonal skills are all qualitites targeted by bullies, as well as characteristics shared by a child with SAD.

The impact of bullying on children with SAD can be significant, intensifying the negative feelings already experienced by the child. This can be particularly true if the bullying happens over a long period of time. It's important for the victim of bullying to report early and get support, something very difficult for the socially anxious child.

How can you help? Teach your child how to report a bully and/or ask for help long before he or she may need to use the skill. Role-play the various methods and practice the skill. Tip Sheet #15 includes some of the components of teaching the skill.

In addition to teaching your child what to do if he or she is bullied, it is important to teach your child interpersonal skills and correct negative cognition cycles, both of which are typically present in children with SAD. Delays in interpersonal skill development, as well as overly negative cognition patterns have been associated with both SAD and increased peer victimization (Erath et al., 2007). Focusing on these key components of SAD can help reduce the long-term aspects of the disorder, safeguard against prolonged SAD symptoms, and reduce potential victimization.

Worksheet #10

The Avoidance Trap

Directions: Complete the worksheet in order to understand your child's avoidance, the reasons for the behavior, and possible interventions.

Event/Activity Avoided	Possible Reasons for the Avoidance	Potential Interventions
Example: *Refused to attend school on the day the teacher was changing the seating chart*	*My child grew anxious in anticipation of the change. She was worried that she wouldn't know the people she had to sit near.*	• *Talk with the teacher ahead of time about changes in routine and work out a plan for my child to have some control/choice within the change* • *Allow my child to be an active participant in the change* • *Practice relaxation strategies* • *Work on lessening threat perception and anticipation*

Review the responses on the worksheet. Are there any themes/trends you are noticing? Anything that needs further examination?

_____

_____

_____

_____

_____

_____

_____

_____

_____

_____

The following tools can be used in conjunction with this one to assist in behavior analysis and intervention development:

- Questionnaire #2: How Avoidant Is My Child? (p. 15)
- Tip Sheet #2: Supporting SAD at School (p. 22)
- Worksheet #9: Understanding My Child's Behaviors (p. 77)
- Worksheet #11: Understanding My Triggers (p. 107)

Tip Sheet #15
How to Report a Bully

- First clarify what a bully is and is not with your child.
- Determine if the school has an anonymous way to report bullying. If it does, allow the child to use that format. If it does not:
  o Determine a "safe" time to talk with the administration of the school.
  o Encourage your child to always report incidents of bullying.

- If your child is the victim of bullying, be sure to spend time teaching the child how to work past the negative impact of the bully.

This book contains numerous examples of specific social skills to teach as well as some strategies to assist parents and educators with reducing a child's negative thought patterns.

Chalk Talk: When Bullying Prevention Programs Fail

Approximately 1 in 3 students report being bullied at school (National Center for Education Statistics, 2013). These sobering statistics have resulted in numerous schoolwide bully prevention programs across the United States. Although most of these programs do create safer school climates, they do not work 100% of the time. It is critical for teachers to create bully-free classroom environments.

Creating a safe environment starts with the clear establishment of rules and expectations. Distinct instructional leadership is also vital to the creation of a safe learning environment. Treat students with unconditional high regard and respect, and expect your students to do the same for one another. Focus on the creation of a caring environment, something I discuss in more detail later in the book.

Tip Sheet #16 includes a few more strategies that will help you create a safe environment within your classroom. Safe and caring classrooms are

Tip Sheet #16

Creating Safe Classrooms

- Discuss and post rules related to bullying within your classroom.
- Treat students and staff with respect.
- Show authentic, positive interest in your students.
- Establish yourself as the clear leader within the classroom.
- Reward positive and inclusionary behaviors.
- Listen to parents and students if they report incidents of bullying.
- Use class meetings to discuss classwide bullying situations.
- Refer students adversely impacted by bullying to mental health staff.

one of the best protection factors you can give to your anxious students. It is also one of the best things you can do to promote greater academic success.

MEET JAYLEN

Jaylen is a recent high school graduate currently attending a community college. We met when he was in seventh grade, after a bullying incident that resulted in significant school refusal. His parents contacted me to help them support their son's attendance difficulties, something that was beginning to result in serious consequences to both him and his parents. During our initial meeting, Jaylen told me that he hated school and felt that most kids only want to bully or torment the "weaker" kids. When Jaylen and I met, he had been identified as a student with exceptional needs due to the presence of a learning disability. His teachers described him as both anxious and unmotivated. He had several discipline citations related to bullying, both as a victim and as a perpetrator.

JAYLEN'S STORY

Jaylen didn't like school. Always feeling like he lived on the fringe of the school culture, Jaylen never identified with a specific peer set. He struggled in ways the majority of his classmates didn't, learning to read at a much later rate than his peers. By third grade, he was identified as having a learning difficulty and was required to take classes to support his reading difficulties.

This was the beginning of the end according to Jaylen, the start of his complete lack of faith in the school system.

Jaylen took special reading classes in grades 3, 4, and 5. The class took place during his regular reading time and happened in a "special lab." Jaylen wasn't the only child to attend the lab, but he felt alone. The other children showed improvement faster than he did. And they weren't teased. At least, not that Jaylen saw.

He was.

Every day at lunch, some kid would taunt him about his reading difficulties. When he was asked to read in class, Jaylen could feel the judgments coming from the other students, heard them gasp when he reached a difficult word.

Jaylen tried not to let the other kids bother him. His teacher always told him about oral reading assignments early, just to give him extra time to prepare. Jaylen took the help and practiced reading the passage the teacher assigned. But it wasn't enough. As soon as he got in front of the class he stumbled on his words—even the words he knew.

His parents hired a tutor to practice more reading skills throughout the week. This didn't seem to help either as Jaylen continued to struggle anytime he read in class or had to answer questions.

Eventually, after trying for more than a year, Jaylen began to give up. He begged his parents to homeschool him. His parents refused. He asked them to send him to a different school; again his parents weren't able to meet the request. Jaylen started missing school, claiming to be sick. Numerous medical tests and a 3-month counseling attempt later, Jaylen continued to voice significant concerns about attending school. The doctors ruled out illness and the counselor said that Jaylen was experiencing anxiety, something not unusual for children with learning difficulties.

In sixth grade, more than a year after he started begging for other options, Jaylen's mother took a leave of absence and began to homeschool Jaylen. She thought that the extra attention she could give him could not only help with the anxiety Jaylen was feeling, but hopefully result in improved reading and learning skills.

The results were initially good. Jaylen willingly participated in the lessons his mother prepared and appeared to be making progress. The stress at home lessened with the loss of the typical school experience and Jaylen appeared to thrive.

Tip Sheet #17

Building Self-Efficacy

- Teach children to recognize and change negative thoughts.
- Teach children how to set goals.
- Notice and celebrate successes, and teach children to do the same.
- Use performance-based praise. Value effort at least as much as achievement.
- Give children an opportunity to take autonomy of their learning.

But the success was short lived. Soon, Jaylen developed a renewed anxiety, causing him more resistance with both schoolwork and the community outings his mother planned with other homeschooling families. Over the course of a few months, Jaylen began to refuse to leave the house without an argument. Unable to continue to meet her son's needs, Jaylen's mother returned him to public school and initiated private counseling. Once again the results were mixed, with early success followed by a significant regression to crippling anxiety. Jaylen's psychologist recommended medications, behavioral therapy, and additional supports within the school setting. By the end of start of seventh grade, Jaylen was receiving services through special education for a learning disability, including reading remediation and additional support in two of his general education classes.

Jaylen and I started working together following an IEP meeting. His parent requested additional supports in the area of self-advocacy and anxiety following an incident of bullying in his special education setting (name-calling and relational aggression) and the subsequent 7-day school refusal. Jaylen and I met weekly for the majority of the year. During this time, we worked on his perceptions of bullies, his confidence, and his self-efficacy (see Tip Sheet #17). The work was slow. With each success, Jaylen backslid into old behaviors, including school refusal. For him, the avoidance had become an engrained habit that proved difficult to break.

Each session focused on his successes and on shifting his perspective. Jaylen eventually learned to accurately self-evaluate following behavioral incidents, correctly identifying his triggers and the way in which he responded to several different types of situations (Worksheet #11). However, Jaylen struggled with anticipating reactions. He was often unwilling to role-play a scenario mentally in preparation for events. This resulted in continued episodes of anxiety and continued school refusal.

Jaylen experienced a significant increase in school refusal during high school, often missing 3 or more days a week. He eventually moved from the traditional high school to a continuation high school before experiencing some success. At the continuation high school, Jaylen was able to better manage his emotions and anxiety. With the assistance of additional therapy, medication, and a strong school-home communication pattern, Jaylen began to regularly attend school and eventually graduated.

LESSONS LEARNED

Jaylen's story, like so many others, epitomizes the difficulties of identification and treatment of anxiety disorders. In this case, Jaylen was wrestling with an underlying learning difficulty that had gone undetected and unsupported for several years. In addition, Jaylen's peers teased him, drawing negative attention to his difficulties. The teasing was not addressed, resulting in poor mastery and confidence for Jaylen. Further, Jaylen's parents were unable to support the core issues of his learning difficulties because they did not understand the depth of the problem. All in all, this case represents a failure on many fronts, all resulting in a significant impact educationally, socially, and emotionally.

I chose to include this case as a reminder that social anxiety is performance related in most cases. Behind the performance difficulties are a variety of potential triggers, including learning problems, social skill acquisition deficits, and more. All of these aspects need to be addressed and supported in order to prevent the scope of the problem Jaylen experienced. Also, this case demonstrates how pervasive the problem can become once avoidance is the habituated response during moments of anxiety.

The take-away message here is to pay attention to the early signs that your child is in distress and seek answers. As parents, I believe you are the best equipped to know your children; you see when they are struggling and recognize their emotional lows more readily in most cases. It is up to you to pay attention to your child's emotional landscape and notice when they are struggling, to seek help, and to continue to ask questions if you are unable to find the answers to your child's problems.

Jaylen's case demonstrates just how quickly a problem can go from manageable to serious. Seek both educational and community resources if your child is struggling with school attendance or verbalizing severe performance

Worksheet #11

Understanding My Triggers

Directions: Complete the worksheet to develop an action plan for each triggering event.

Trigger	My Response	Action Plan
Example: The teacher called on me in class.	I got scared and started to tell myself that everyone was going to laugh at me.	• Take a deep breath • Tell myself I can do what the teacher has asked • If needed, ask for a break • Complete the task

Now, take a moment and write a few words or sentences to describe any roadblocks you worry may occur as you try to implement your plans.

_____

_____

_____

_____

_____

_____

_____

_____

_____

anxiety *before* he or she becomes too entrenched in the difficulties. It is often uncomfortable to reach out, especially if the professionals you turn to do not share your concerns. But keep at it; your child is relying on you.

Concluding Thoughts

The impact of social anxiety is unmistakable, affecting everything from a child's ability to meaningfully participate in class, to building social relationships, to coming to school with consistency. Children with social anxiety perceive schools to be a hotbed of threats, something that educators and parents may struggle to understand. There is no logic to the perceptions, only fear.

It is important for parents to recognize and understand the ways in which social anxiety may be impacting their child. This understanding will enable parents to work with the school to build a caring environment that supports the child and helps him or her correct faulty thinking and build the habit of working through the anxiety. These are important skills for the child to master in order to gain control over his or her social anxiety.

Although I believe that the school environment often elicits the strongest negative reaction in children with SAD, it is not the only way in which socially anxious children are impacted. The next chapter will focus on the impact of social anxiety on peer relationships. This, too, can be an area of significant impact for our children with SAD.

CHAPTER 6

Social Anxiety and Friendships

"Social anxiety impacted me very heavily both at home and in the classroom. Every time I would get into an argument with my parents, I would never explain why I was upset. It wasn't because I didn't want to, I just didn't know how. I didn't want to make them angrier so I kept my mouth shut. In the classroom it was even worse. I hardly ever made friends at school, I never raised my hand and had a lot of trouble working in groups. Group work was a nightmare for me. I always dreaded it because that meant that I would have to talk to other students and attempt to collaborate with them. I didn't like getting bad grades so I had to make sure that they didn't do bad work on whatever it was we were working on.

I also struggled with making friends and telling others how I feel. Being a girl, it was extremely difficult talking to boys without thinking that they were judging me in some way. It made me feel like I would never be able to settle down in the future and have a family of my own." —Female college student with SAD

Chapter 5 examined the impact of social anxiety on school performance and functioning. Chapter 6 will take a closer look at the impact of social anxiety on the development of friendships.

The Importance of Friends

Human beings are social animals. Our social development is an essential aspect of who we are. What our friendships look like may change based on age, development, temperament, and social conditioning. That does not change the important role of peers and the development of friendship.

As children, friendship formation is often highly influenced by parental involvement. We determine which people our children associate with, set up play dates, and help our children through difficult friendship drama. When our children demonstrate socially anxious behaviors, we are often available to help coach our children through their difficulties and encourage them to join in activities and develop at least one or two friendships.

Often we don't see the significant impact of social anxiety on our children until they begin to exhibit extreme behaviors in response to our insistence that they connect with others. Maybe we worry about shyness or introversion, not understanding that these behaviors are different from social anxiety. So we work and work to help our children develop friendships without addressing the underlying anxiety and fear our child has not yet been able to communicate.

As children enter early adolescence, the influence of parents begins to wane. Friendship expectations grow increasingly more complex. Peer relationships diversify into webs of close friends, groups based on interests and romantic relationships. The increased expectations and complexities of peer interactions often leave the socially anxious child unable to cope, triggering an increase in avoidant behaviors.

With less influence over a child's social behaviors, a parent's role as the primary emotional support for a child shifts. Children begin to depend on their peers for emotional support. This can pose unique problems, as discussed in Chapter 5. Often the child with SAD will gravitate toward other peers with similar avoidant and anxious tendencies. Neither child, in this scenario, possesses strong social skills, putting them at risk for increased peer victimization. This can be especially true when both children demonstrate social anxiety (Biggs, Sampilo, & McFadden, 2011). As mentioned throughout the book, the best protection factor against the negative impact of SAD on friendship development is to address the underlying features of social anxiety, including poor social skill development and faulty thinking.

It is easy to see the difficulties of developing friendships for the SAD child. These same difficulties apply to larger peer groups, including academic groups. Children with social anxiety struggle to feel accepted within a group. Their underdeveloped social skills put them at risk for rejection. This, in turn, results in increased withdrawal or avoidance, which further prevents the acquisition of skills. The cycle repeats significant deficits in social competency results.

Tip Sheet #14, Building Social Competency (see p. 98), addressed a few ways to build social competency within the context of school. The same strategies can work within any social group. The more we can foster growth in social skill acquisition, the more we can buffer anxious youth from some of the negative results of social anxiety.

Social Information Processing Model

Weak social skill development is only one of the factors that adversely affect peer relationships among socially anxious children. Cognitive biases also play a role in the difficulties many children with SAD experience.

One way to examine cognitive biases and the impact on social interactions is to use a social information processing model. Developed by Crick and Dodge (1994), social information processing refers to the way in which children develop successful relationships. This model consists of four stages that include encoding specific situational cues, interpreting the cues, searching for responses, and selecting a specific response. These stages loop together in a fluid model.

For the child with social anxiety, difficulties can occur in any stage of the model, from encoding to responding. As indicated in the first section of the book, children with SAD often overemphasize threat cues from the environment, selectively attending to them over neutral or positive cues. Furthermore, socially anxious individuals often focus on their own actions to the expense of recognizing subtle cues within the social environment or seeing the bigger picture and different perspectives of the situation (Biggs et al., 2011). These cognitive biases can skew both the encoding and the interpreting of social cues, adversely impacting the anxious child's ability to develop successful friendships.

Social anxiety also influences both response analysis and selection, as individuals with SAD tend to overemphasize threat and engage in increasingly negative thought patterns, which skew their responses. The result is an unsuccessful social encounter, perpetuating the negative cycle.

It is important to address these difficulties with cognitive biases in order to improve a child's social processing. Worksheet #12 can guide you as you begin to coach your child with regard to his or her social processing. Analyze the specific missteps your child is making and strategically address the problems. The more success, no matter how small, your child can begin to achieve, the more positive momentum you can build.

Adolescence, Dating, and SAD

As mentioned previously in this chapter, adolescence represents a period of increasing complexity in peer interactions as teens begin to date and form romantic relationships. This can be particularly difficult for socially anxious teens.

Like successful friendships, healthy romantic relationships serve as protection factors for adolescence, offering esteem enhancement and social support (La Greca, Davila, Landoll, & Siegel, 2011). For the teen with SAD, however, romantic relationships can be difficult to form. More often, socially anxious teens engage in avoidant behaviors and withdraw from dating and social events. The lack of "practice" at forming relationships leads to increased skill deficits and withdrawal. A cycle similar to the one already discussed often follows as anxious behaviors become habituated.

Some children with social anxiety do form romantic relationships. However, the relationships often offer less social benefit as they lack the intimacy and positive qualities of typical relationships. The negative dating experiences lead to avoidance and the cycle starts again. The key to breaking this cycle involves correcting the cognitive biases and addressing the underlying social deficits as indicated throughout the book. More than anything, it is important to help.

No conversation about teen dating is complete without mentioning the proclivity of dating victimization. Current statistics indicate that

Worksheet #12

Understanding My Child's Social Processing

Directions: Following the example and the information from Worksheet #2: My Early Warning Signs (p. 13), complete the following chart about your child's stress, the way your child is interpreting triggers, and potential interventions.

Stages	My Child's Actions	Potential Interventions
Encoding situational cues: Initial situation introduced	*Example:* Teacher calls on my child in class.	N/A
Cue analysis: Interpreting cue as threatening or neutral/positive	*Example:* Situation is perceived as threatening by child.	*Example:* Work on perception and changing perspectives. Use Worksheet #3: Threat Discernment (p. 30).
Response search: Deciding which response should be taken	*Example:* Based on past experiences, my child may yell, leave the class, cry, or stay silent.	*Example:* With a new perspective, I can encourage my child to look for new choices, including asking for help and asking for a break.
Response selection: Choosing a response	*Example:* My child began to cry and asked to go to the nurse.	*Example:* I taught my child to ask for a break next time, or better yet to ask for help with the question as needed.

10% or more of adolescents report being hurt by their romantic partners (La Greca et al., 2011). Dating abuse can lead to increased social anxiety and can further maintain existing occurrences of SAD.

Like bullying, it is critical that teens are taught about appropriate and inappropriate relationships, as well as instructed on how to talk to someone about dating victimization. Tip Sheet #18 may be useful in providing specific ways for teens to talk about dating abuse.

SOCIAL ANXIETY AND LGBT YOUTH

The research regarding social anxiety among LGBT youth is scarce. This is particularly unfortunate considering that SAD occurs at a significantly higher rate among adults who are LGBT (Roberts, Schwartz, & Hart, 2011).

Reasons for the increased rate of social anxiety among LGBT youth are unclear. However, some research suggests that gender nonconformity at a young age coupled with negative attitudes toward LGBT youth increase feelings of anxiety in children within the LGBT population. These negatives attitudes are frequently verbalized within school settings, often setting the stage for increased incidents of peer victimization and abuse. This is particularly true with transgender youth (Roberts et al., 2011).

LGBT youth report feeling different from their typical peers at a young age. This feeling of being an outcast happens not only at school, but within the home setting as well. Significant fear of rejection is reported among LGBT youth among both those who disclose their sexual identity and those who withhold disclosure (D'Augelli, Grossman, & Starks, 2008). Increased childhood abuse is reported among LGBT youth, including abuse that occurs within the home environment (Roberts et al., 2011). All of these factors put LGBT youth at increased risk of developing social anxiety, depression, and suicidality.

The need for increased support for our LGBT youth is clear, both in the home and school settings. Support at home can start with open acceptance of our LGBT sons and daughters. This acceptance is critical for our children to develop a sense of belonging within the family structure.

Acceptance is not limited to the home setting. Schools must focus some of their antibullying efforts on supporting LGBT youth. Zero-tolerance for harassment and verbal or physical aggression needs to be established for the LGBT youth community. Given that many LGBT youth report missing school for fear

Tip Sheet #18

Talking About Dating Abuse

The idea of dating abuse and victimization is a scary one for most parents, and an uncomfortable topic for both children and parents. To help recognize dating abuse and help support your child, it is important to maintain open communication with your adolescent. Here are some tips for talking to your teen. These tips will also set the stage to enable your child to talk about the abuse.

Before your child starts dating (if possible):
- Talk with your child often.
- Work on developing your relationship first.
- Create a caring and open relationship with your child.
- Be aware of how you refer to and react to domestic violence.
- Regularly talk about difficult subjects including respect, sexual activity, boundaries, anger management, and the differences between healthy and abusive relationships. Keep the communication on these topics open and avoid sounding judgmental or "preachy."

If you suspect abuse:
- Express your concerns without judgment.
- Be supportive and open. Use active listening techniques.
- If your child asks for help to get out of the relationship, help him or her develop a safety plan.
- Make sure your child knows you love him or her regardless of the situation.
- Help your child find help from a counselor, therapist, or group (in person or online) to support him or her.

of safety and bullying, it is vital that schools make this a priority (Roberts et al., 2011).

Treatment for socially anxious LGBT youth is somewhat different than treatment for other SAD populations, with an increased focus on developing coping strategies as opposed to correcting faulty thinking. This is because most of the negation expressed by LGBT youth is based on real-life experiences and not misperceived threats. Additionally, therapies utilizing cognitive behavioral therapy and exposure techniques dicussed in the later chapters of the book have been found to be effective in the treatment of SAD.

The important take-away lesson with LGBT youth is tolerance and acceptance. Much of the increased prevalence of anxiety disorders among this population results from society's lack of acceptance of this specific population. It is this lack of acceptance and support that ultimately results in an increased prevalence of social anxiety and more extreme mental health concerns, including suicide.

Chalk Talk: Creating a Culture of Caring

Few things have more of an impact on a child's learning than the classroom environment. Creating a culture that supports the needs of diverse students, increases tolerance, fosters healthy relationships, and supports prosocial behaviors should be the first goal of any teacher.

But how can a teacher create such a culture of caring within the classroom?

The answer is surprisingly simple. Start with the establishment of clear rules and expectations that are taught to all students. Then, establish a nonverbal signal to get the class's attention. Implement a classwide positive behavior management system in which the behavior expectations are explicitly taught, modeled, and reinforced. Embed social skills training into your curriculum. Use icebreakers and team building activities prior to group assignments.

All of these strategies will support all students within your classroom environment. Tip Sheet #19 recaps the process for your quick reference. A caring culture is one of the best ways to mitigate the negative impact of anxiety concerns.

MEET RICKIE

Rickie, born as Ricardo, is a fifth-grade student who is transgender. She has significant social anxiety and often refuses to engage in school. She acts out in class, refuses to attend some days, and struggles with the social venue

Tip Sheet #19

Creating a Caring Environment

- Develop clearly defined rules and expectations.
- Have predictable routines.
- Focus on positive interactions.
- Provide space and time for learning.
- Balance the needs of diverse learners: group activities for extroverts, solitude for introverts, enrichment and remediation, etc.
- Cultivate prosocial skills among your students.
- Maintain open communication with parents and students.
- Have unconditional high regard for your students.
- Know your limits and the limits of your students.

of school. I began working with Rickie when her parent, a single mother, was charged with not bringing her child to school. At the Student Attendance Review Board hearing, Rickie's mother indicated that Rickie was dealing with many "difficult" problems that were impacting her ability to attend school. She and I met the following day and she explained that Rickie was dealing with transgender issues and social anxiety that had developed previously. Rickie and I spoke after my meeting with her mother. She stated that although she was biologically a boy, nothing about her "felt" like a boy. She said she was trapped in the wrong body, and everyone hated her for it.

RICKIE'S STORY

Rickie was born feeling different. From her earliest memories, she considered herself a girl, despite being born male. She preferred traditionally feminine toys, was fascinated with playing dress-up, and cherished her dolls. Everything about her felt feminine, except her biology. Her mother reported that Rickie's earliest self-drawings depicted herself as a girl, something her mother readily admits was alarming.

Rickie's mother thought she was going through a phase related to the lack of a male figure at home. She encouraged Ricardo to "act like a boy." She enrolled him in sports, continued to dress him as a boy, and sought out male role models. When it was time to start school, Rickie's mother enrolled him as Ricardo, the boy to whom she had given birth.

Rickie lived as Ricardo for 9 years. She calls these years the hardest, worst years of her life. She wanted to please her mom and tried to be the boy her mother wanted. But she hated it, and soon she started to act out. She cried anytime her mother took her shopping or forced her to participate in "boy" activities. She corrected her teachers when they called her Ricardo, telling them that she liked the name Rickie.

By third grade, her friends began to notice that she wasn't a typical "boy." She liked to hang out with the other girls. In fact, most of her friends were girls. When she asked about play dates, it was always with other girls. Her drawings continued to represent Ricardo as a girl. At home, she played dress-up and told her mom that she was tired of "pretending" to be a boy.

In fourth grade, Rickie refused to hide any longer. She told her teacher to call her Rickie and stated that she was a girl. Her friends laughed. Another boy teased her and the girls were afraid. Her teacher said Rickie was confused and called her mother.

Rickie was ashamed. She went to the nurse, pretended to be sick, and begged her mom to change schools. She even threatened suicide. Her mom didn't know what to do. She consulted her priest, who stated it was a phase once again. Unsatisfied, she consulted her doctor. He referred her to a therapist who specialized in transgender issues among children. It was then that Rickie's mother learned that Rickie could be a transgender child.

Rickie changed into a new school for fifth grade. Her mother enrolled her as a girl and hoped no one would ask any questions. At first, things were fine. Rickie was allowed to dress as a girl. The school made arrangements for her to use the bathroom in the nurse's office. No one seemed to know or care that Rickie was biologically male.

A month into the year, Rickie's classmates began to suspect that Rickie wasn't a typical girl. Within a few weeks, they started teasing her on the playground. Rickie's mother complained, and the bullying got worse. All of Rickie's previous fears returned. She started calling her mom from school, stating she was sick. She stopped performing in class. Her grades dropped drastically, and Rickie missed more than 3 weeks of school.

It was at this point that I met the family. Rickie's mom told me Rickie's story. Rickie shared her shame and guilt about causing so many problems for her mom. She stated that she didn't mean to hurt anyone, she just didn't know how to be a boy and was tired of lying.

Tip Sheet #20

Talking Students Through "Mini-Vacations"

Directions: Use this tip sheet as a guide to teach your child or student how to take a "mini-vacation." Ask the child to sit in a comfortable chair. Then read each of these statements to the child. Watch as the child goes through the steps, paying particular attention to the outward signs of stress your child may exhibit. Do not move to the next step without seeing the beginnings of reduced stress with the child.

- Close your eyes and take several deep breaths.
- Quiet the chatter in your thoughts.
- Focus on your favorite place to relax. For me, it's the beach.
- Imagine everything about that place—what it looks like and the sights, sounds, and smells of the place.
- Focus on nothing but this place as you take a few more deep breaths.
- When you are calm, open your eyes.

My work with Rickie focused on the anxiety related to her transgender difficulties. I spoke with her therapist monthly, reporting any progress or setbacks. For the most part, the work centered on building self-esteem, self-advocacy, and acceptance. Specific visualizations were taught to assist Rickie when she was feeling overwhelmed. Rickie particularly liked both breathing colors and the mini-vacation exercise (see Tip Sheet #20). She said that she could do these techniques in class without people knowing what she was doing.

In addition to learning relaxation strategies, Rickie and I worked on her perceptions of self. Although Rickie had been taunted and bullied at her previous school, she had not endured the same level of torment at her current school. In fact, she had made both male and female friends in her class. Despite the progress with her peers, Rickie continued to view herself as a socially inept outcast. Our work focused on challenging that opinion of herself and replacing the negation with something more accurate and more positive.

Rickie has made great progress over the last several months. As she enters secondary education, her mother has indicated significant concerns regarding Rickie. Certainly, the increased peer pressures in secondary education pose unique challenges. In an effort to be proactive in dealing with the concerns, a counseling plan was developed for Rickie with a goal of addressing the necessary social skills as she begins middle school. Rickie is encouraged, though understandably hesitant about her upcoming years.

LESSONS LEARNED

LGBT youth pose unique educational challenges, especially as related to social competency and SAD. Rickie's case was included as an example of the complexities of dealing with LGBT cases. Parents and educators are dealing with increased numbers of transgender cases at younger and younger ages, as our youth are finding ways to more openly discuss their gender and sexual identities. With increased disclosure comes increased potential for peer problems and social anxiety, something both parents and educators will need to come to terms with.

It is important that we take a moment to understand our own feelings about LGBT issues early. Review the quiz presented earlier in the chapter and understand your personal biases before you confront the LGBT issues you may be faced with at home or within the community.

As stated earlier, any condition that threatens the status quo has the potential for setting off often serious anxiety-related behaviors in our children. Knowing your own personal biases regarding the more controversial triggers of anxiety, including LGBT issues, will help you navigate these difficult waters as you find the balance between supporting and nurturing your children, mitigating any social anxiety concerns, and preparing your children to live in a world that isn't always forgiving.

Concluding Thoughts

The social milieu can be difficult for most children to navigate from time to time. This is even more true when you are a child with social anxiety. Fears related to being humiliated by peers can paralyze a child and keep him or her from developing the very skills needed to gain social competency and prevent the development of SAD. Interventions that focus on developing healthy connections and correcting inaccurate threat perception continue to be the key in helping manage social anxiety when it impacts friendships.

This chapter highlighted several of the most common issues that arise within peer interactions, including dating and issues unique to LGBT youth. In the next chapter, the impact of social anxiety as children move into the world is discussed, including the impact within the family, mental health concerns, and suicidal ideations.

CHAPTER 7

Social Anxiety in the World

"When my daughter was 6 or 7 years old, we attended a large family gathering at her grandmother's home. This was a place where she spent a lot of time and [she] was comfortable there. When we arrived, she walked up to the front door, looked in, and turned around and walked away. Nothing anyone said or did was going to make her go in there with all of those people. When I realized what was going on, I suggested that she go around the house and play in the backyard. She agreed, and the rest of us went in and visited with the family. She did come in the back door later to use the bathroom and to get some food, but she never really visited with anyone. She was quite happy when it was time to go home.

A lot of people thought that I made the wrong move on that one. I should have forced her to go in. I should have forced her to be polite. I should have forced her to behave. What they didn't know is that I did force her far beyond what she wanted to do. She didn't want to be there at all. I also knew that if I had forced her to go in the front door, it would have been by me carrying in a kicking and screaming child. They didn't know what we were dealing with." —Parent of a daughter with social anxiety

Social anxiety can affect every setting, causing significant stress to the family unit. This chapter examines the stress social anxiety places on siblings and parents, as well as some strategies to reduce the intensity of social anxiety.

SAD and the Family

By now it should be very clear that social anxiety affects more than the person feeling the anxiety. Social avoidance and the resultant behaviors, both internal and external, can wreck havoc on the household. Siblings are challenged as the socially anxious child demands more and more of the parents' time. Parents are stressed as they watch one of their children suffer with anything social.

As discussed in Part I, social anxiety is sometimes seen within multiple members of the family related to genetic and environmental factors. Anxious parents, for example, often raise anxious children. Having multiple members of the household struggling with anxious behaviors can often result in increased strain on the family unit. This strain serves as its own maintenance factor for social anxiety, as the increased conflict results in more avoidance and delays in problem solving.

It is important for the parents of socially anxious youth to evaluate their own levels of anxiety and establish a family household that fosters prosocial behaviors, relaxation, strong and caring relationships, and clear boundaries. All of these factors will work to minimize the negative impact of social anxiety and improve overall outcomes.

Before parents can move toward a supportive household environment, it is important for parents to determine the current state of functioning. Questionnaire #6 can help parents determine the current strengths and challenges of the household, as well as the ways social anxiety is currently affecting the home environment. Regular completion of this worksheet will help you determine which strategies are working for the entire family.

Once strengths and challenges are identified, it is important to target one or two challenges for change. Don't overwhelm the household by changing too much at once. One or two small changes can often yield big results. Utilize the various interventions presented throughout the book to correct the areas you've selected.

Keep in mind that your particular parenting style will significantly impact the effectiveness of various interventions. Adapt strategies as needed in order to yield the results you are working toward.

Questionnaire #6

My Household Inventory

Directions: Read each statement as it relates to your household and decide if you agree or disagree with the statement. For additional benefit, allow each household member to complete a copy.

	I agree	I disagree	I neither agree nor disagree
Each person in the household knows the expectations or rules.			
The rules have meaning to the members of the household.			
Each household member knows the consequences for breaking a rule.			
Consequences are consistently applied.			
Every household member knows his or her role in the family structure.			
Each member of the household respects the boundaries of the others.			
Parents are predicable consistent in their reactions to the children.			
Household members have chores and know what the chores are.			
Children participate in some of the decisions in the household.			
Every member of the household has opportunities to contribute to the running of the household.			

Looking through the questionnaire, what do you notice? Is there disagreement between any of the household members? Are there areas that need clarification? Take a moment to jot down your thoughts.

_____

_____

_____

_____

_____

The Role of Parenting Style

As mentioned elsewhere, parenting styles significantly influence both the development of social anxiety and the continuation of anxious behaviors. Understanding your specific strengths and challenges as a parent is vital if you want to create an environment that can support your child's anxiety and minimize the negative effects.

Revisit Questionnaire #5: What's My Parenting Style? (p. 49). Are your answers still reflective of your parenting style? Are there specific aspects of your parenting style that work? Are there things you'd like to change? In Worksheet #13, make a list of the aspects of your parenting you'd like to target for change and indicate what the change should look like. Repeat this activity anytime you feel like the household is not supporting your children's behavior.

Providing Equal Time

Few things are harder than parenting a child with unique needs, except meeting the needs of multiple children. Sibling rivalry is an unavoidable outcome of households with multiple children. Children will naturally pull parents' attention in order to get needs met, establish hierarchies, and develop social skills. Sibling rivalry can be particularly problematic when one or more of the children struggles with social anxiety.

One of the most common arguments among siblings relates to fairness. When a child feels unfairly treated as compared to another, the child's anxiety may increase (Campione-Barr, Greer, & Kruse, 2013). This belief stems from the child's perception and is influenced by how the child encodes cues, perceives threats, and responds. It is easy to see that the child with social anxiety will likely see more acts of unfairness than a nonanxious child, regardless of the truth of the situation. Correcting a child's cognitive biases is vital to preventing an escalation of sibling conflict within the household.

When sibling conflict does occur, which it will, it is important for parents to remain as neutral as possible, while focusing on consistent expectations, boundaries, and consequences. Tip Sheet #21 can help you

Worksheet #13

Thinking About My Parenting

Directions: Take a moment to reflect on your specific parenting style. You can refer back to Questionnaire #5: What's My Parenting Style? (p. 49) if you need help recognizing your parenting habits. Complete this chart, highlighting those aspects of your parenting you would most like to change.

What I Am Currently Doing	What I Want to Do Instead	Action Plan for Change
Example: I panic when I see my child cry because I know that the crying usually leads to a full meltdown.	I want to remain calm and not automatically anticipate a problem, but remain proactive.	• Take four deep breaths • Tell myself to be calm • Adjust the environment or our plans in order to calm my child • Alternate activities if needed • Ask for help as needed

Tip Sheet #21

Sibling Conflict Management

The following strategies can help redirect sibling conflict and restore peace:
- Start by teaching respect, responsibility, teamwork, and empathy.
- Hold regular household meetings.
- Maintain open lines of communication between all family members.
- Teach conflict resolution skills.
- Establish quality one-on-one time for parents and each child, as well as time for siblings to spend together.
- Hold all children responsible for their own behaviors.
- Defuse feelings of jealousy quickly.
- Acknowledge each child's point of view and don't take sides.
- Ignore the small arguments.
- Get involved in the large problems that involve any form of victimization.

navigate the difficulty of sibling rivalry in ways that enhance each child and develop prosocial conflict resolution skills.

SOCIAL ANXIETY, DEPRESSION, AND SUICIDAL IDEATIONS

Few things scare parents more than the possibility of severe depression and suicide among their children. As discussed in Chapter 4, depression has a high comorbidity rate among socially anxious children. Looking at the long-term impact of social anxiety, it is clear to see how depression can develop.

Children with social anxiety struggle with peer interactions. Despite wanting friendships, many youth with SAD are unable to successfully navigate the social world. Unable to develop close friendships, they begin to withdraw and a significant negative cycle begins. This cycle sets the stage for the development of depression, as the avoidance of others, rumination on negative effects, or the negative perception of events and feelings of hopelessness increase.

Feeling sad is a normal thing. However, sometimes the sadness slips into depression and may be an indicator of a severe problem. The list below includes typical indications of potential depression. If these things are experienced persistently over time or form a consistent trend, it is important to seek the help of a skilled professional:

» Persistent mood of general unhappiness and/or sadness
» Loss of interest in previously enjoyable activities/things
» Decreased energy
» Change in sleep patterns
» Change in appearance
» Change in weight and/or appetite
» Suddenly teary and/or emotional
» Unable to think clearly or concentrate
» Feelings of hopelessness and worthlessness
» Feelings of helplessness
» Suicidal ideations

Figure 3. Indicators of potential depression and potential suicidal thoughts.

There are many things parents can do to minimize the negative aspects of SAD. First, find ways to connect your child to the family unit and at home. Focus on strategies presented throughout the book, including helping to correct faulty thinking and teaching social skills. Finally, understand the warning signs for depression and suicide. Figure 3 includes the signs of depression and suicide. If you are concerned that your child may be contemplating suicide, please take him or her to a skilled professional for an evaluation as soon as possible.

The long-term negative impact of social anxiety is clear. But with your support and assistance, children dealing with SAD can have significantly improved outcomes.

Chalk Talk: Supporting Families Dealing With Significant Mental Health Issues

Few things are more difficult than helping families in crisis. This can be particularly true when supporting a family dealing with mental illness. There is a lot of shame and negative stigma attached to mental health concerns. The general public continues to view mental illness as a matter of choice. As an educator, you may even be guilty of viewing the issues facing your student as a matter of bad parenting or choice. I encourage you to not take that road.

Every day I receive questions or comments from parents struggling to cope with their child who is exhibiting serious mental health issues, including depression, mood disorders, and severe social/behavioral disorders. These parents feel isolated, lonely, and ashamed. Like the public around them, they tend to blame themselves for their child's illness. In the case of true mental illness, it is highly unlikely that the parent is *directly* responsible.

Supporting parents as they work to find ways to support their mentally ill children involves tolerance, empathy, and compassion. It is important that neither the parent nor the child be shamed as they seek help. Work with the parent to determine what needs the child has at school and secure assistance. Treat the parent and child as you would like to be treated in the same situation.

There may be times when supporting the parent is difficult. Perhaps you do not fully agree with the diagnosis presented to you. Or maybe the behaviors you observe at school are drastically different than those reported to you by the parent or within the independent evaluation. If this is true, you have a few options—believe and support the parent, regardless of your personal feelings or dig your heels in for what you perceive is right. My advice? Support the parent and child, regardless of much else.

This doesn't mean that everything the parent requests is something you can do. It may not be. But you can always come to the conversation from a position of compassion and support. Work with the parent, utilize support from the mental health professionals on campus, and find a way to help the child.

If you stay focused on building relationships with the parent and child, then you will be able to move past any differences and help the child, regardless of your personal feelings about the specific situation.

MEET TRINITY

Trinity is an African American student attending a comprehensive high school. At the time I met her, she exhibited several oppositional behaviors, including verbal aggression, violating school rules, and school refusal. Her disciplinary record indicated problems that started in middle school. After a few weeks working together, it was clear that Trinity was dealing with more than bad behavioral choices.

TRINITY'S STORY

I met with Trinity and her parents following a suspension for leaving class. Trinity had an extensive disciplinary history that included chronic truancy, aggression, and noncompliance. She had been identified by the school administration as a student with significant behavioral problems. Teachers and administrators expressed concern over her constant defiance, walking out of class without permission, truancy, and task refusal. Needless to say, her parents were more than a little concerned about the potential for expulsion.

Trinity's school history indicated disciplinary concerns in middle school that included verbal altercations. In high school, the problems escalated to include physical aggression. A review of her educational records indicated a history of poor work completion, task refusal, and inconsistent attendance.

A full psychoeducational evaluation was completed for Trinity in seventh grade due to concerns about attention deficits and possible emotional struggles. Results indicated average overall abilities, low average academic skill development, and significant oppositional behaviors. The team ruled out attention problems and emotional disturbance, stating that low motivation and oppositional behaviors were the causes of her educational difficulties.

In the years that followed the assessment, Trinity continued to struggle with her work. She began to skip school and resisted most attempts to obtain compliance with class and school rules. Homework was seldom completed. Despite the lack of practice, Trinity passed most district and statewide assessments.

At home, Trinity's parents characterized Trinity as helpful around the house. She followed the majority of the household expectations. Her parents also reported that Trinity became defiant when asked to participate in social events with her family or when discussing school performance.

Trinity had goals of being a doctor when she was in elementary school. By the time I met Trinity in high school her only goal was to be finished with high school so she could "live her life in peace," as she put it.

Trinity and I started to work together as part of a school-based assistance plan to prevent expulsion. She was told that one more violation of the school rules would result in potential expulsion.

Trinity came to me dressed appropriately. She was animated when she talked, as long as the conversation was focused on things she wanted to discuss—future plans to go into cosmetology with a goal of working in the film industry. When the topic switched to academic performance, Trinity's behavior changed. She withdrew, often shifting her body away from me. It took nearly a month before she was willing to open up about her middle school experiences.

Trinity perceived middle school as the beginning of her problems. She stated that she was one of the few African American students at school. She further stated that people didn't understand her. They considered her loud. When she presented information in class, her peers were disinterested. Trinity reported that her classmates seldom engaged with her in discussions they way they did with other students. Most interesting was Trinity's opinion that she could never please the new social group.

One day, according to her, she gave up on trying to please them or gain their acceptance. She stopped editing her words and challenged those who gave her dirty looks. Before long, she began to physically respond to what she perceived as threats. Trinity explained that she was regularly treated unfairly, further breaking any positive connection she had with school.

After talking time to understand Trinity's perspective, it was clear to me that many of her behaviors originated out of a fear of not being able to connect with her new peer group. The isolation lead to additional maladjusted behaviors. Although Trinity demonstrated significant problems maintaining her behavior, as well as a significant lack of motivation, the cause was not strictly behavioral.

In my opinion. Trinity was coming from a place of faulty beliefs and fear. She was afraid of being humiliated so she used her behavior to protect herself from this perceived threat. In doing so, she further distanced herself from any positive connections at school, reaffirming her fear. The negative cycle had begun.

I knew I had to help her connect to something, anything, positive at school if I was going to have any hope of helping her. I started a check-in/check-out process with her.

Trinity checked in with me every morning. We reviewed a behavior contract, discussed her goals, did an exercise related to her faulty thinking, and I sent her to class. The meeting was 15 minutes or less every morning. Trinity checked in again at the end of the day. We reviewed her contract, discussed the day, and focused on a gratitude journal entry for the day. Together, we developed a positive thought for the next day's focus and she went home. Trinity was then required to review her progress with her parents.

Initially, Trinity was somewhat reluctant to participate. But she knew she had to try or risk suspension and expulsion. Within a month, Trinity was able to find something positive each day. In 2 months, she could develop positive affirmations with no prompting. By the end of the school year, Trinity began to set goals.

It's been more than 7 years since I first worked with Trinity. A phone call with her family several years ago indicated that Trinity had decided to attend a cosmetology school and was currently living with friends. Her mother reported that she seemed happier, although she continued to struggle with forming positive friendships. Trinity opted not to pursue therapy outside of school to work on correcting faulty thinking and understanding her fears. Although her parents were disappointed by Trinity's choice, they did report that Trinity was doing well overall.

LESSONS LEARNED

It would have been easy to write Trinity off as a statistic, a lost girl uninterested in school. Her overly aggressive behavior, poor attitude, and low motivation screamed that she wanted people to stay away and leave her alone. Fortunately, her parents didn't listen or give up. They wanted more for their daughter, no matter how hard she pushed them away.

Trinity's case points to the need to continually investigate the underlying causes of apparent behavioral problems with a critical eye. It is important to pull good histories and thoroughly interview parents and students.

Trinity's case also points to the importance of creating positive cultures within the school setting. Taking time to connect with disenfranchised youth is critical to changing behavior and improving outcomes.

Although I am fairly certain that Trinity's case involves at least some degree of social anxiety, Trinity was never formally diagnosed with SAD. The interventions I utilized were ones I felt could be effective with not only behavioral challenges and resiliency concerns, but also with social anxiety.

Which brings me to the last important aspect of this case: I've stated repeatedly that SAD seldom happens alone and cases are often complex. It is important for everyone working with socially anxious children to utilize global strategies that can address myriad issues. Many times what works for a case of SAD will also work for a behavior problem and for a child with indicators of depression.

Concluding Thoughts

The last three chapters have focused on the impact of social anxiety in terms of school, friends, and the family. Children wrestling with SAD are forced to confront their deepest fears on a daily basis, sometimes without understanding or support. My hope is that these chapters have shed some light on this impact and offered practical ways to support those struggling with social anxiety.

The next section focuses on helping our children navigate through the world of social anxiety. There is hope for these children. Correcting cognitive biases and establishing a new normal in which the world is not so scary is something that can be achieved.

PART III

Creating Safe Havens

CHAPTER 8

How to Help

> *"Both of my children suffer from social anxiety, my daughter more than my son. I find myself in the odd circumstance of coaching them to do some things (like call an acquaintance from school, for example) that I could never actually do myself. I don't want them to be as lonely as I am at my age, though, so I want to encourage their social skills to the best of their capacity while they are still young (they are teenagers). As for me, I am lonely. I would like to have more friends but don't know how to make them. So I spend most of my time alone (or with my teens)."* —Jocelyn, an adult with SAD parenting children with social anxiety concerns

We've covered a lot of ground in the first two sections of *Raising the Shy Child*, addressing both the symptoms and the specific ways social anxiety may present itself. Now it is time to shift focus and look at the specific ways to help our children with SAD. The next three chapters will review various types of evidenced-based treatments for social anxiety, as well as the specific ways parents can understand and assist in supporting their anxious children.

The overriding feeling expressed by the parents of socially anxious children is one of loneliness and isolation. Parents feel like they are the only ones to truly understand their children. Maybe teachers have repeatedly told them there is nothing wrong. Or maybe parents have been made to feel overprotective. Or maybe parents have been too ashamed to reach out for help. Regardless of why and how it happens, many parents feel completely helpless, scared, and alone when it comes to supporting and reversing the negative impact of social anxiety in their children.

You may feel the same way.

The good news is that you are not alone. Not even close. School personnel, support groups, and mental health professionals are available to assist you as needed. But sometimes, knowing how and when to access help is the biggest hurdle.

First, Do No Harm

Watching your child suffer from social anxiety is very difficult. If you were (or are) someone who suffered from social anxiety, your child's behavior will likely open up your own wounds and fears. In turn, your own fears ignited, you may decide that giving in to the fear is required in order to calm down the anxieties. So you let your child miss school or a party ("just this once"). Maybe you allow your child to avoid talking to the family members who always elicit an anxious response. Or you allow your child to consistently hide from big family gatherings.

All of these allowances are done with the best of intentions—to provide a respite of safety and calm for your child. And at first it may appear to work. Your child may seem happier and better able to function. That is, until the next party or school day comes. Having successfully avoided the activity once, often with a positive result, the child's avoidance was reinforced. This all but guarantees a repeat performance. Each time the child is allowed to completely avoid the anxious trigger, the child is told "you are right, this *is* a scary thing and you *don't* have the skills to deal with it, so you get to avoid it."

I'm fairly certain no parents want to give that message to an anxious child. They don't want their child to grow up believing he or she should be anxious. But when we support a child's fears by allowing the avoidance, that is exactly what we are doing. Over time, this will lead to increased anxiety and further habituation of the very response we want to eliminate.

Another way in which our choices as parents cause more harm is by our own styles of parenting. As discussed in Chapter 3, there is a correlation between parenting style and the development of social anxiety. When parents are overprotective of children without explanation, the subtle message is "the world is something to be feared." Likewise, when we discuss all of the potential dangers with our children, without providing context or strategies for dealing with the real dangers that exist in the world, we overemphasize both fear and threat. This distorted point of view negatively reinforces the child's already present fear and says "yes, you are right to constantly be afraid."

The key to working with the socially anxious child is to first remain calm. Work through your own issues and fears prior to working with your child. The more calm you are, the more convinced you are that your child will work through his or her anxieties, the more able the child will be to balance his or her own fears.

Your child will always look to a parent or trusted adult to gage how he or she should react in various situations. If you give in to your fear, if you see threats around every corner, and if your child's own fears terrify you, then your child will be more fearful as well.

Questionnaire #7 can help you monitor your own thoughts, fears, and beliefs. It is important to review these questions periodically to ensure that you have managed your own emotions before attempting to help your child.

Working Within the System

As I mentioned at the beginning of this chapter, parents regularly express a sense of loneliness and isolation when dealing with their socially anxious children. I hear comments like "No one knows what I'm going through, how hard it is to cope" and "I am all by myself in this." Nothing is further from the truth. Anything, even social anxiety, that impacts a child's ability to learn is absolutely something that concerns the school. In fact, it is the school staff's responsibility to assist a child with social and emotional difficulties when these difficulties impact educational performance. In the case of social anxiety, there is almost always a negative school impact.

As discussed in Chapter 5, schools are typically very impacted by social anxiety. And given the prevalence of SAD, it is not as unusual as you may believe for a parent to seek help from the school in this area. This is particularly true if the social anxiety is impacting the child's ability

Questionnaire #7

Thinking About My Emotions

Directions: Ask yourself the following questions to assist you in managing your emotions and behaviors before you help your child. Then teach your child this same strategy to help him or her manage his or her behaviors and emotions.

1. What happened?

   _____

   _____

2. What was I feeling at the time? Was I afraid? Anxious? Angry?

   _____

   _____

3. Did I lose control? Did I *feel* like I would lose control?

   _____

   _____

4. Am I calm now?

   _____

   _____

5. Did I use any strategies to calm down? How effective were they?

   _____

   _____

6. What did I notice most about my behavior and emotion?

   _____

   _____

7. What worked for me this time? What should I do differently next time?

   _____

   _____

Tip Sheet #22

Soliciting Help

Asking for help can be difficult, especially if you are dealing with your own levels of anxiety. The following considerations and questions will help you and the teacher work together to help your child.

Considerations:
- Start with mutual high regard for the teacher and educational staff, assuming that everyone is working for the good of your child.
- Discuss your concerns in clear and specific terms. Try to remain emotionally neutral.
- Develop mutual goals and a plan for working with your child that can be consistently implemented across settings.
- Discuss a time to review your child's progress.
- If there is disagreement, work through the concerns with an open mind, focused on meeting the needs of your child.

Questions to get the conversation started:
- Do you notice my child exhibiting any anxiety-like behaviors?
- Is my child willing to socialize at school?
- Is my child willing to speak in front of the class?
- Has anyone ever laughed at my child during class?
- What does my child do at recess or lunch?
- Do you have any concerns about my child's functioning?

to attend school with consistency, or participate in his or her education when he or she is at school.

But how can a parent access help?

The first step is to speak openly with the teacher about the social anxiety. Explain the impact both at home and with reference to school. Ask the teacher what, if anything, she sees within the school setting. The list of questions in Tip Sheet #22 gives you a place to start with the teacher. Modify this to meet your specific needs. Each question is designed to help both you and the teacher get the information you need to help support your child.

Often, the teacher has similar concerns as the parent. In this case, the teacher may suggest holding a meeting with a team of teachers, support staff, and administrators. These meetings, often called Student Study Team or Student Success Team (SST) meetings are held for the purpose of brainstorming ways to support and assist the child. They can be called for everything from academic concerns, behavioral concerns, attendance concerns, or anything else a parent or teacher feels would benefit from this type of brainstorming session.

SST meetings typically end with the development of specific strategies to assist the child. The team agrees to meet at a later date, usually within 6–8 weeks, to evaluate the success and effectiveness of the interventions. The team may also adjust interventions and move to more significant types of interventions at the follow-up meeting. Figure 4 gives you a typical example of interventions you may develop through the SST process for a child with social anxiety. Most schools will attempt these interventions readily without additional assessments or paperwork other than what is utilized by the school through the SST process.

When the interventions are not as successful as the team would like, a decision may be made to conduct some form of an assessment for consideration of accommodations and support through either Section 504 of the American with Disabilities Act (ADA) or through the Individuals with Disabilities Education Improvement Act (IDEA, 2004).

Students with social anxiety could potentially meet eligibility for additional support through Section 504 and/or IDEA. Which level of support is required for the individual student is determined by looking at the specific nature and impact of social anxiety on the particular child's educational functioning, including academic and social development.

Section 504 is a civil rights law that ensures that individuals with a disability (as defined under Section 504) be provided equal access at work, at school, and throughout the community. In educational terms, the law provides for equal access to education. The law defines a student with a disability as a person with a physical or mental impairment that substantially limits major life functioning in areas that include caring for one's self, walking, seeing, breathing, and *learning*, to name a few. The law also states that a person with a disability has a "history" of the disability and is "regarded" to have that impairment (U.S. Department of Human

Accommodations for students with social anxiety are developed to mediate the fear of being embarrassed or humiliated at school. Some typical accommodations include the following:

- » Seat the student next to a calm, helpful peer.
- » Develop and use nonverbal signals to alert the student to directions on the board or those given orally.
- » Develop and use nonverbal signals to tell a child that his or her turn to answer a question is coming. When possible, set the student up for success, allowing him or her to answer questions on confident topics.
- » Allow for flexible methods of showing mastery.
- » Allow for flexible testing conditions to mediate anxiety.
- » Establish safe zones during recess and lunch for the student.
- » Establish a safe person on campus to help coach and mentor the student.
- » Provide advanced warning (as possible) of changes in routine, fire drills, and teacher absences.

Figure 4. Typical accommodations for anxiety.

and Health Services, n.d.). Mental health concerns including anxiety disorders (like social anxiety), are eligible for support through Section 504 when the impact of the condition limits the student's learning.

Section 504 is considered highly inclusive legislation and educators are encouraged by the U.S. Department of Education and the Office of Civil Rights (OCR) to focus not on the eligibility aspects of 504, but on the ways in which the educational environment can support an eligible student.

To the student with social anxiety, Section 504 is a potential option for support when the interventions already offered through the SST process are not yielding the desired result. Figure 4 indicates the typical types of interventions found on a Section 504 plan. These plans offer some measure of protection under federal law, ensuring a level of interventions be available to your child as needed.

Occassionally the supports offered through Section 504 are not enough to support your child. Maybe your child's anxiety has resulted in significant school refusal, problems functioning within a typical classroom despite several layers of interventions, and signficant problems with emotional control. In these cases, you may want to consider your options under IDEA.

Developed to protect students with disabilities and provide for access to the typical curriculum, IDEA is the most restrictive form of legislation protecting students with exceptional needs. Eligibility for special education through IDEA is determined through a psychoeducational assessment completed by a team of highly skilled professionals that may include a school psychologist, special education teacher, and other specialists.

In the case of social anxiety, potential eligibility for special education services can be found under the eligiblity criterion for Other Health Impaired (OHI) or Emotional Disturbance (ED). Additional services including counseling and mental health support are available when the degree of social anxiety is so significant that it completely disrupts the child's ability to learn within a typical classroom setting.

This information regarding SST meetings, Section 504, and IDEA was presented with the assumption that the teacher sees the same impact of social anxiety to the child as you do. As unfortunate as it is, this is not always the case. What can you do if the teacher does not see the same adverse affects of anxiety as you do?

In this case, I think it is very important to attempt to work through any differences of opinion with the teacher first. Sometimes things that hugely impact the home setting do not at all impact school. When this happens, it is important to seek support for the difficulties in the home setting, either through therapy or other mental health and coaching avenues. If there is no impact at school, monitoring your child's academic progress may be all that is initially warranted.

If there is true disagreement regarding the negative or harmful impact of social anxiety on your child's academic functioning, and you cannot come to a compromise regarding support, you can go to the school administrator for assistance. Additionally, many schools have a school counselor or psychologist that may be able to help. The important thing to remember is that you are not alone in this. There are people to help.

The upcoming chapters will address ways to access therapeutic help and the best evidence-based treatment options.

Tip Sheet #23

Social Skills at Home

Review Figure 2: Critical School Social Skills (p. 96). That list included several essential social skills for success. This list provides additional insight to the social skills most attributed to developing social competence.

- Communication skills, including initiating friendships, articulating needs and wants, and accepting "no" for an answer.
- Self-soothing skills, including remaining calm, learning to relax, and flexible problem-solving skills.
- Mindfulness, including learning to quiet inner noise and discerning actual from perceived threats.

SOCIAL SKILLS AT HOME

I've talked a lot about the need for specific teaching of social skills within the school setting, especially because research indicates that many children with social anxiety struggle in this area, adding to the negative impact of the anxiety. However, social skills aren't only for school. There are several skills needed at home too.

Encouraging the development of strong social skills in the home setting is not difficult. Begin by talking with the child about the need for developing social competency and social skills. Make a list with your child of the different skills needed in everyday life. Tip Sheet #23 has a few of the skills I focus on with families.

Once you and your children have decided on the list of skills important to your family, pick one skill to focus on at a time. You can change these weekly or every other week as your children develop competency with the skill.

The next step is to teach the skill. Talk it over with your child. Come up with examples of what the skill looks like and what it doesn't look like. Think about when the skill should be used and how it makes you feel when it's used correctly. Once your child has a good working understanding of the social skill, it's time to role-play scenarios in which the skill will be used. Take turns being the person using the skill.

Finally, it's time to practice the skill in real life. Plan a few occasions when your children can utilize their newly learned skills. Praise their performance when they are successful and gently redirect them when they need guidance. At the end of the day and week, review the skills learned and your child's progress. Feel free to use incentive charts as appropriate.

That's it. Once you get into the habit of practicing social skills at home, you'll wonder why it took so long to get started. Refer to Tip Sheet #13: Teaching Social Skills (p. 97). The more you practice these skills, the more help you are providing to your children to protect them against social anxiety and more.

Chalk Talk: The Hard Talk

Teachers are often the first people to recognize a problem with a child. When the problem is more than academic concerns, it can be difficult to know how to bring up the topic with parents. But, no matter how hard it is, educators need to express their concerns.

The best way to start a difficult conversation with parents is through a parent-teacher conference. Conducted in private, this affords the teacher an opportunity to address concerns in a safe and somewhat comfortable environment.

Sometimes inviting the school psychologist or school counselor can help both the parent and the educator feel more comfortable. Skilled at making people feel more comfortable during sensitive conversations, mental health educators can often provide additional information and strategies to the parent and teacher, easing the concerns of all involved.

No matter how apprehensive an educator may feel about addressing sensitive topics with a parent, it is important to not let a situation drag on too long before bringing it to the parent. If you, as an educator, are recognizing a problem, the odds are that the parent is as well. Regardless, waiting to discuss difficult subjects typically makes the conversation more difficult.

Tip Sheet #24 reviews a few pointers for making the conversation a little easier. Review this list any time you need to open the lines of communication on difficult subjects.

Tip Sheet #24

The Hard Talk

Talking openly with parents about children and concerning behaviors can feel like a daunting task. These tips may help make this a little easier:

- Start from a place of mutual high regard and respect.
- Present the facts and keep opinions to a minimum even if requested.
- Be aware of your tone and body language.
- Be open and honest with parents.
- Focus on solutions, not problems.
- Be brief but thorough.

MEET MIKAYLA

Mikayla is currently a middle school student struggling with anxiety characterized by avoidance and extreme threat perception. I began meeting with Mikayla at the request of her parent due to ongoing concerns about her negation and its impact on her educational functioning.

MIKAYLA'S STORY

Mikayla and I met when she was in third grade, and continued to work together until she transitioned to middle school a few years later. Her parent and teacher referred her to me due to ongoing concerns about her lack of engagement at school and nearly continuous negative perceptions of school, friends, and her life. Most days Mikayla failed to complete her assignments, was reluctant to participate in class, and appeared to have few friends. When her mother asked her about her day, the majority of her answers were negative.

I interviewed Mikayla on three occasions prior to my work with her. In each of our sessions, Mikayla's conversations centered around the negative outcomes of social situations. She would tell me how she and a friend had fun playing only to come back into class and have the friend ignore her. Or how she went to a party and had fun, but the other girls weren't very nice. No matter what the initial topic of conversation, Mikayla consistently found a way to bring the focus back to something negative. This pattern of seeing the world as one large threat permeated everything, often increasing Mikayla's reluctance to work.

Mikayla and I spent a lot of our initial time together speaking about school and her lack of engagement. Mikayla told me that she often refused to work because she knew she couldn't do the work so she'd rather not try than risk continued embarrassment.

Mikayla's mom indicated that Mikayla had always been a reluctant child. She was highly cautious around unfamiliar people as a child, crying with almost anyone other than her mother.

Mikayla's mother also described Mikayla as a "fussy" baby, often reacting negatively to the subtle changes in the environment—lights that were a little too bright and sounds that were too loud. Mikayla's sensitivity continued and worsened as school began.

Despite her pessimistic view about school and the world, Mikayla initially performed well in kindergarten and first grade. In second grade, Mikayla started to complain about going to school. She said that she knew it was going to be a "rough" day, so she didn't want to go.

Her parents took her to the doctor who advised them to get Mikayla to school at any cost. As a result, she seldom was absent, but her negation increased. In third grade, she started to miss school, leading to our work.

My initial goal with Mikayla was to improve her coping skills and reduce negative belief patterns. I believed that cognitive biases were at the core of Mikayla's difficulties. Indeed, Mikayla herself admitted that she felt that the majority of her day was destined to be bad and that anything good that could possibly happen would be a mistake and was not to be trusted.

Mikayla and I spend more than a year working on perceptions, changing her belief structures and coping skills. I started a gratitude journal with her and asked her to find two positive things daily (see Tip Sheet #25). This was initially very difficult for Mikayla. But after about 3 months, she was able to accept that the world was not exclusively negative.

Our work also consisted of training Mikayla on the skills of asking for help, stating something positive about a situation, and accepting "no" for an answer. I felt these skills were needed in order for Mikayla to improve in her peer interactions and reduce the negation.

Over the next 18 months, Mikayla made significant progress. Mikayla's mom recently reported that although Mikayla still engages in pessimistic thinking, she is more positive overall and engages in school with more consistency. She no longer requests to stay home and is earning appropriate grades.

Tip Sheet #25

Using a Gratitude Journal

1. Make a special section in a journal or notebook to use as a nightly "gratitude" journal.
2. Every night before bed, write 3–5 things you are thankful for. These need not be big things. They can be as simple as being thankful it didn't rain. Anything, really.
3. Do this every night until you've developed the habit of looking for things that bring out your grateful heart.
4. For an even bigger impact, share your gratitude journal with others daily.

LESSONS LEARNED

I included this case as an example of how quickly a small problem can overtake a child's life. For the first few years of school, Mikayla made good progress at school. She engaged in negative self-talk frequently, but the negation did not appear to adversely impact her daily functioning.

As the social and academic demands of school increased, Mikayla's coping mechanisms failed. She was no longer able to move past her negation. Everyone experiences this breakdown in coping strategies at some point. For Mikayla, it was earlier than expected.

Getting Mikayla on track and reducing the impact of her negative thinking and threat perception was a matter of teaching her to refocus on the positive as opposed to the negative. Additionally, receiving a little training in biofeedback enabled Mikayla to *feel* the impact of her stress and adjust her moods. Finally, improving her social skills taught her how to ask for help and engage with peers in a positive way. This further reduced the impact of her anxiety and eventually reduced her negation.

Concluding Thoughts

It should be apparent after reading this chapter that there is help for parents of children with social anxiety, both through the educational system and by utilizing mental health services. Educational supports including SST plans, Section 504 accommodation plans, and even IDEA can be utilized to minimize the negative educational impact of social anxiety. Accessing these programs requires knowledge and persistence at times. It isn't that educators don't want to support children with anxiety-based difficulties. More likely, educational teams don't always understand the degree to which supports can be offered. Hopefully through this and similar books, both parents and educators will be able to craft individualized plans that can help our socially anxious youth.

The next chapter will tease out ways to understand and support the behaviors associated with SAD, from avoidance and withdrawal to oppositional and tantrum behaviors. The presented approaches and strategies can be utilized through the plans discussed here as well as within the home setting.

CHAPTER 9

Developing an Action Plan for Home

> *"I do not have social anxiety. However, one of my really good childhood friends suffers from this. She is shy and uncomfortable in larger social groups, but also has a love of conventions and other large social gatherings like festivals. Throughout the year, I've gently tried to pull her out of her shell and be the support she needs. The road hasn't been easy for her. I remember one time I had to rush into the city just past midnight, because she was having such a severe panic attack that she stopped breathing and had to be rushed to the emergency room."* —Amy, friend of an adult with social anxiety

One of the most typical ways to support a child's behavior at school is through positive behavior support (PBS) planning. PBS principles typically identify behaviors targeted for change, proactive ways to reduce the need for the behavior, replacement behaviors we'd like the child to use and how to reinforce the use of the positive behavior, and what to do when the child is engaged in the problem behavior anyway. Research has shown PBS to be highly effective at reducing negative behaviors and increasing prosocial behavior in a variety of school and residential settings (Metzler, Biglan, Rusby, & Sprague, 2001).

Although this type of behavior planning typically occurs within school settings and with externalized behaviors, the basic principles can easily be adapted for use within the home setting and with behaviors typical to social anxiety, including withdrawal and school phobia.

This chapter will explore the basic elements of positive behavior supports and their application in the home setting.

Assessing Need

Before any positive behavior supports can be developed, it is critical to understand the specific needs of the child and what behaviors should be targeted for support. Start by reflecting on everything you have learned about social anxiety and your child by this point. What stands out to you most about your child's specific social anxiety and its impact? Are there specific behaviors you feel are related to the anxiety that you want to change? Take a moment to complete Worksheet #14, focusing on no more than two or three behaviors initially. How does the behavior look at home? At school? In the community? Does the behavior change based on the environment? What about other people—does the behavior change based on who is around? Once you've completed the worksheet, focus on one or two behaviors only. I recommend that parents focus on the most problematic thing first. School or task refusal is usually the place to start.

Step 2 involves determining *why* the child is engaging in this behavior. Most behavior happens as a way to get something (e.g., attention, a specific tangible, prestige) or to avoid something (e.g., attention, a task, a specific thing). Go through the behaviors above and complete the second step. What is your child trying to get or avoid through the behavior?

Sticking with the school refusal example, perhaps the child is avoiding a particular class or type of activity. Or perhaps he or she is seeking the attention you provide when he or she misses school, even if that attention is negative. Write down your thoughts as to the "function" of the behavior on Section 2 of Worksheet #14.

Once you've isolated a behavior or two to target and determined why you think your child is doing these things, it's time to test your theory a little bit. If you think your child is engaging in behavior to get something, make sure it doesn't work—deny the child the thing he or she is

Worksheet #14

Behaviors to Change

Directions: Complete the worksheet to develop an action plan for each behavior you'd like to change.

Description of Behavior	What Is the Probable Goal of the Behavior	Behavior You Would Prefer to See	Skills Needed to Reach Goal Behavior
Example: My child begins to cry when I drop her off at school.	She is scared of being at school and wants me to take her home.	My child gets out of the car, says goodbye, and goes into school without crying.	• How to communicate her frustration without crying • Self-soothing • Positive self-talk

Now, take a moment and write a few words or sentences to describe any roadblocks you worry may occur as you try to implement your plans.

_____

_____

_____

trying to obtain. If you are correct about why the child is engaging in the behavior, then he or she will either increase the behavior to get what he or she wants or try something else.

Through this process you can refine your opinion as to why the child is behaving a certain way. Another way to refine your thoughts on function is to closely look at what happens just before and just after the behavior. This can tell you both what triggers the behavior and what reinforces the behavior to continue. Both will give hints as to the behavior's function.

Consider the child who resists going to school. Most days you can coax her to attend, but whenever the day starts with a test, she blows up, throws a tantrum, and refuses to go. As a result, you are typically late and she misses the first hour of school. In this case, the trigger is the test at the start of the day. Her behavior, the tantrum, serves to communicate her need/desire to avoid the test. The bigger the tantrum, the later she arrives to school, and the more likely she is to miss the test. If she does manage to avoid the test, her behavior is reinforced, and you can expect her to try this pattern again unless something is done to prevent the cycle.

Sometimes it is difficult to determine exactly what the cycle of behavior looks like. In these cases, keeping a behavior journal can help. Worksheet #15 reviews an easy way to maintain the journal, including what types of things to record.

Proactive Interventions

Once you have isolated both the behavior and probable function of the behavior, it is time to look at the environment. The goal here is to reduce the child's need to engage in the problem behavior.

Although you assessed your child's behavioral needs, you also isolated some of the triggers for the behavior. These triggers hold the key to mediating the child's need to engage in the problem behavior. If your child engages in avoidant behavior every time he or she has to give an oral presentation, you know that the act of giving the presentation is the trigger. The next question is, what can you do to make giving an oral presentation less likely to trigger the behavior? Notice I never said the plan

Worksheet #15

Behavior Journaling

Directions: Take a look at the chart below. Complete each section as indicated in the example. For every behavioral incident that occurs, consider what happens immediately before the behavior, as well as immediately after. Then try to determine why the behaviors may be occurring. Most of human behavior happens to enable use to get or escape/avoid something. Think of possible meanings to your child's behavior in these terms. At the bottom of the chart, indicate any anecdotal information such as the setting or other factors for consideration.

Date/Time	Behavior	What Happened Before the Event (Context)	What Happened After	Possible Meanings for the Behavior
Example: May 15; 8:45 a.m.	My child threw a tantrum (yell, scream, kick).	I asked her to get in the car and go to school.	I attempted to pick her up and put her in the car.	She didn't want to go to school. She was afraid of going to school.

Anecdotal notes:

_____

_____

_____

_____

_____

is to avoid the trigger. You already know that avoiding anxiety negatively reinforces it. Instead, the goal is to reduce the impact of the trigger.

There are a few ways to achieve the goal. Typically, changing how the child perceives the trigger will have the best result. This can be achieved in a variety of ways. Sticking with the example above and the oral presentation trigger, perhaps the impact of the trigger would be lessened by giving the oral presentation to a friend or the teacher instead of the class. In this way, the environment has been adjusted to reduce the need for the problem behavior (the need to avoid the oral presentation). The child still has to give the presentation, but not in front of everyone. You've found a way for her to fulfill the task without triggering the meltdown.

Let's go through another example of how this can work within a home setting. Let's say that your daughter becomes highly anxious during family parties. The anxiety is demonstrated by her increased defiance whenever the house is full of people, even when the people are familiar. The cycle of behavior starts with the party, increasing episodes of defiant behavior from your daughter, eventually resulting in her being grounded and sent to her room. In this example, the defiance clearly serves the purpose of escaping the party. The trigger is a large gathering, and the reinforcement of the defiance is being grounded.

Reducing the impact of the party to your child would be a great proactive goal in this scenario. But how? I would start with determining how many people your daughter can tolerate—4, 6, 10? Once you know that information, begin to have parties that are only that size. Expect her to participate for a while before she can request to go to her room. Slowly increase the size of the party until you reach the typical size. In each case, allow her to leave the party without having to misbehave in order to do so. At the same time, teach her how to both tolerate more people and ask for a break. I will address ways to teach these new skills in the next section.

Mediating the environment to support the needs of the child does not mean avoiding triggers or overprotecting your child. It simply means understanding where your child is currently functioning and slowly building his or her tolerance and willingness to accept something different.

Teaching New Skills

Once you've reduced the number of times your child engages in the behaviors you are trying to support by supporting the environment, it is time to teach new skills. This is the most critical aspect of behavior training—and one that is not always completed.

In the case of socially anxious children, there are several skills that likely need to be taught, including discerning and correcting faulty thinking, social skills, and relaxation. Although all of these are very important and ultimately needed, this section refers specifically to teaching your child what you would like her to do *instead* of the inappropriate behavior. In the example of the child who is resistant to attend school when there is a test or an oral presentation, you may want to teach the child how to ask for help or how to verbally express his or her fears. In the case of the child becoming defiant in order to avoid a party, you may want to teach the skill of asking for a break or expressing the condition of being overwhelmed.

Teaching children specific skills can be done in a variety of ways. For most children, the best way to teach a new social skill (like the ones above) is to directly teach the skill in simple steps, role-play the skill, have the child repeat the skill, and then practice the skill. I've given two examples of basic social skill teaching scripts in Tip Sheet #26. These examples, adapted from common PBS strategies, provide a basic framework of each skill and an easy to remember way to teach the skill.

Once the skill has been taught, it is critical to provide performance feedback whenever the skill is used, commenting on what went well and where refinement is needed. Positively praising successful use of the skill is also necessary in order for the child to begin to use the skill.

When It All Goes Wrong

Sometimes even the best of intervention plans will fail and our socially anxious children will engage in the behaviors we are trying to reshape. It's important to anticipate this possibility and have a plan to

Tip Sheet #26

Social Skills Scripts

Developing a script or guideline for the specific aspects of various social skills can feel like a Herculean task. However, once you have a little practice, it's easy. To help you get started, I've included two typical social skills and scripts. The first one is good to use with a younger child, while the second can work with preteens and teens. I've included a little role-playing scenario for the first skill to demonstrate how these steps work.

Accepting "no":
- Make eye contact with the speaker.
- Listen clearly.
- Don't interrupt.
- Say "I understand."
- If you disagree, speak later when everyone is calm.

Problem solving:
- Start with respect.
- State your position clearly.
- Manage your emotions.
- Offer solutions, not just problems.
- Listen to others without interrupting.
- Don't argue.
- Be flexible.

Parent-child dialogue example:

Parent: Jessie, today we are going to practice the social skill of accepting "no." Can you think of a time when it is important to accept "no," even if you don't want to?

Child: Yes. When you tell me "no" about staying up late, I should listen because you just want me to get some sleep and don't want me to get sick.

Parent: Is it sometimes hard to accept "no"?

Child: It's very hard.

Parent: I know it is. Here are a few steps that will make it easier to remember how I want you to behave when I have to tell you "no." First, I'd like you to look at me when I am speaking to you, Next, I want you to listen to what I say without interrupting. At the end, I'd like you to say "Okay" or "I understand." If you need me to hear your side of things, please wait until we are both calm. Can you repeat the steps for me please?

Child: (Child repeats the steps)

Parent: Now, if you forget some of the steps, I will be reminding you so we can practice the skill, okay?

Child: Okay.

It's important to review and practice the steps frequently. In time, your child will begin to accept "no" for an answer in most situations.

help your child regain his or her emotional balance. This is called a reaction plan.

Reaction plans begin with making sure *you* are staying calm. Take a moment to collect your thoughts and relax yourself before attempting to help your child relax and regroup. Once you know you are calm, it's important to get your child back to his or her baseline of functioning as quickly as possible. This can often be achieved using de-escalation language, reminding the child that he or she is safe, and reminding the child what you'd like him or her to do.

Using the example of the child who is refusing to attend school, the reactive plan may focus on reducing the size of the tantrum while also insisting on school attendance. This can be an emotionally difficult thing to accomplish. However, failure to return to the expected behavior will wind up reinforcing the child's engagement in the problem behavior and may undermine all of your hard work. Remember, it should be expected that the child will mess up and return to the targeted behavior from time to time. It is important to plan ahead, push through the crisis, and move forward.

Tip Sheet #27 provides a few guidelines for working with the problem behaviors and returning the child to a baseline as soon as possible. The important thing to remember with a reactive plan is that the child is resorting to previously learned behavior because it worked! It's critical

Tip Sheet #27
Working With Behavior Explosions

- Emotionally detach from the immediate crisis.
- Take a moment to calm yourself first. Then, remind your child how to calm him- or herself. For this to work, you need to have previously practiced this social skill.
- Debrief from the outburst once everyone is out of the crisis.
- Give your child space and time to decompress.
- Reevaluate the current supports your child is using. Determine what, if any, additional social skills teaching is needed and develop a plan to provide that teaching to your child.

that the behavior be less effective than it once was if you are going to help your child redirect to the new, more desired behavior.

After the crisis of the moment has ended and your child is calm, you will want to debrief with your child and help him or her understand what happened that led to the behavior misstep. This may include reviewing the new skill you'd like to see, as well as talking about any consequences for the behavioral problem.

Asking for Help

This chapter has focused on all of the aspects of behavioral planning within the home setting. At first read, it can appear overwhelming. I promise that once you get used to viewing behavior in the ways described throughout this chapter, it will get easier to develop plans and help reshape your child's behavior. To make things a bit easier and provide you with a little cheat sheet, I've developed a brief chart (see Figure 5) that can help you remember what each aspect of a plan entails.

There are times when supporting behavior is too difficult to attempt alone, times when the behavior is complex or when there are many factors influencing behavior. At these moments, it is important to seek help from skilled professionals. This may include educators (including teach-

Stage of Behavioral Crisis	Actions to Take	Goal
Before the crisis	» Teach your child how to manage his or her emotions » Learn the warning signs of your child's escalation cycle » Teach your child how to relax	Prevent escalation from occurring
During the crisis	» Detach emotionally from the crisis » Remain calm » Keep safety in mind » Ignore minor problems	Manage the problem behavior safely and de-escalate the crisis as soon as possible
After the crisis	» Debrief after everyone is calm and the crisis is over » Review strategies for managing emotions with your child	View the crisis as a teachable moment and determine an action plan to prevent future problems

Figure 5. Behavior support planning.

ers, school counselors, or school psychologists), community resources (including pastors and life or parenting coaches), or mental health professionals (including counselors, therapists, and doctors).

Asking for help may feel intimidating at times. Remember, the professionals are here to help you in this process. You are not alone. The next chapter will go into more detail about accessing mental health professionals, as well as the most typical types of evidence-based therapies used when working with socially anxious youth.

CULTURAL INFLUENCES ON SOCIAL ANXIETY

No conversation about social anxiety is complete without a conversation about cultural influences on behavior. Specifically, Western cultures tend to idolize more individualist, autonomous, and personal success-oriented behavior. Eastern cultures, especially Asian cultures, tend to place a higher value on the collective interests and value group efforts over personal success.

This consideration is relevant when considering the impact of diagnosis and potential negative impact among various culturally oriented groups (Holly & Pina, 2014; Zerr, Holly, & Pina, 2011). Similarly, different values placed on social interaction within cultural groups may also impact the definitions and prevalence of social anxiety within a particular subgroup.

Cultural biases have not been widely studied with regard to the development and treatment of SAD. However, research does suggest that children socialized in ways that are different from what their society values are at greater risk of developing mental health concerns, including SAD, often engaging in more withdrawal and avoidant behaviors as a result of the mismatch between the child's native culture and acculturation into the host culture in which he or she is living.

What can parents do to mediate the impact of cultural differences and impact of social anxiety? The key, I think, lies in accepting the cultural impact in the first place. Once acceptance is achieved, I think it's important to understand the specific role culture has on the child's specific anxious behaviors. Finally, adopting a more pluralistic and tolerant point of view is vital in helping culturally diverse children. Teaching that same tolerance at home, in our schools, and within community groups is equally important in order to support the anxiety many of our culturally diverse youth demonstrate as they attempt to find their place within our society.

Chalk Talk: Simple School-Based Support Plans

This chapter has focused a great deal on the development of behavior support plans within the context of home. This same process is used by most educators to create plans for use in the classroom room.

Yes, I know, you don't have time to create behavior plans. You are "just" a teacher after all; you need to focus on reading, writing, and math. I would suggest, however, that focusing a little of your time on behavior planning will help you create the culture within your classroom necessary to your students as they learn.

Creating supports to help your more anxious students doesn't need to be a difficult thing. It begins with observing and understanding the

Tip Sheet #28

Writing a Classroom Behavior Plan

- Establish mutual goals for the meeting with the parents and the plan itself.
- Discuss strengths of child before looking at the concerns.
- Discuss one to two problems only. Problem-solve possible reasons for the behavior and potential.
- Decide on measureable goals for the team and the child.
- Keep it simple. Include how new behaviors will be taught to the child and by whom.
- Revisit the plan often to monitor progress.
- Maintain consistent and clear communication between home and school to assist with both the plan management and generalization of new skills into different environments.

behaviors your students exhibit that get in the way of learning. For most of your anxious students, this will include avoidance and task refusal. It may even include escapist behaviors like leaving the classroom or refusing to turn in work. All of these behaviors can be targeted for support.

Tip Sheet #28 presents step-by step instructions for creating simple behavior plans for students that can have high impact in your room. Follow the process to support the behaviors you most frequently see. If you need assistance with interventions or anything else, consult with your school psychologist or behavior support team. The key is taking a positive approach and teaching your students how you want them to behave.

MEET MATEO

Mateo was student in seventh grade who recently immigrated to the U.S. He worked with me for a few months following a meeting to address significant attendance concerns and dropping grades. Mateo moved from El Salvador and spoke minimal English. He received support for language development, but spent the majority of his day in an English speaking environment with facilitated instruction from an English development instructional assistant.

MATEO'S STORY

Mateo smiled as he came to my office. New to our school, and our country, Mateo appeared to approach life with a happy disposition and hope in his eyes. He seemed comfortable around others and was more than willing to jump into a new situation and give his best efforts. So why was he missing school and struggling?

Mateo came to the United States 2 years prior to our meeting. His family was new to the country as well, immigrating with the hopes of finding more opportunities for their son. Mateo's parents supported the school and took attendance seriously. But when Mateo slowly began to refuse to attend school, they were at a loss.

Mateo and I began working together as part of an agreement between the school and the parents after an attendance hearing was filed. At the hearing, the parents indicated that Mateo said he was scared to come to school. His parents, fearing that Mateo was being bullied, allowed him to stay home for nearly 2 weeks at a time. When Mateo had accumulated more than 40 absences within the semester, the hearing was scheduled.

I interviewed Mateo over two sessions. Mateo came to each session. He was cooperative and willing to talk to me about school and his absences. Mateo stated that while he tried to make friends, he was generally rejected at school. He felt like the other children had no interest in his culture or history. They expected him to be like them, and when he wasn't, they rejected him.

When asked about his acculturation, Mateo stated that his family was traditional and wasn't like Americans. He wasn't supposed to express ideas as openly as children within the American culture did, at least not to adults. He went on to state that he didn't talk to his teachers about concerns he had with the other children, but that "isn't what children were supposed to do."

Mateo said that he learned to keep to himself more and more, despite his outgoing nature. He felt that no one would understand him. After disengaging in school for several months, he decided not to attend at all, stating that it was easier to "just not show up" as opposed to dealing with the negative attention he received from his peers throughout the school day.

My work with Mateo consisted of both reframing his thinking and working with the other students in the class. I approached the seventh-grade teachers about starting a culture awareness program. Through sensitivity training in every classroom and introducing a South American club to the campus, Mateo found a way to celebrate his heritage while still acclimating to his host culture.

Mateo learned how to request help and engage with peers in a positive manner. The other children learned how to be a positive influence on the creation of a tolerant culture within the classroom and school. A win-win scenario.

I only worked with Mateo for a few months before his family moved. I do not know how Mateo's life may have changed after the move, but I do know he left with a new set of skills that had the potential of better preparing him for life's experiences.

LESSONS LEARNED

I included this short case study about Mateo only to highlight some of the influence culture has on our children and the potential for social anxiety. Although I do not believe Mateo's behaviors were strictly indicative of social anxiety, his school refusal was prompted by negative peer interactions and the impact of rejection from his peers.

This case highlights the importance of tolerance training, not just for the children experiencing social anxiety, but for all students. The more open and tolerant the school environment, the more we can actively negate some of the factors that contribute to the development of SAD and reduce their impact on our youth.

Concluding Thoughts

Understanding the communicative intent of behavior takes practice to achieve. However, once you're able to understand what need your child is trying to meet through his or her behavior, you will be able to help your child reshape that behavior, often with great results. With socially anxious children, understanding the intent of behavior often means looking past the extreme avoidance and oppositional behaviors in order to discover where cognitive biases and threat perception are morphing perception. It also means helping your child retrain his or her perception.

I know, this sounds difficult. And it is—at first. But it will get easier. Your child will get better.

Some children will experience significant improvement in their overall anxiety management just by utilizing the strategies and interventions discussed in this chapter. Others will require more intensive interventions. Chapter 10 focuses on the types of help available through the mental health field, as well as how to access the help. Evidence-based treatment options are also discussed. I hope this information will give you the knowledge you need to secure the most appropriate help for your child.

CHAPTER 10

When to Seek Additional Help

"Within the last year I saw a therapist to talk things out. It was very difficult to start talking to a complete stranger about my deepest thoughts. I struggled my way through it, and after a few sessions I was diagnosed and put on medication. Before I went to therapy, I searched the web for some other stories similar to mine. I knew I couldn't have been the only person to be struggling with social anxiety but I had never met anyone else like me. After many months of research, I diagnosed myself with social anxiety. I confirmed it with my therapist and that was when I was put on medication." —Brittany, an adult who has struggled with social anxiety since childhood

As indicated in the previous chapter, helping your socially anxious child can be exhausting. Feelings of isolation and helplessness are not uncommon among parents of socially anxious children. Fortunately, there are many types of professionals who can help.

This chapter will explore the more typical types of professionals and therapies proven to work with SAD, as well as how to make your partnership with the professional work.

Admitting the Problem

By far, the biggest barrier to help I encounter when working with families is admitting the severity of the problem. No one really wants to confront a serious mental health challenge. Most of the time it is easy to minimize the real impact social anxiety is having on the child and on the family. However, failure to recognize the true nature of the problem can also result in a delay of treatment and possibly an increase in negative outcomes of social anxiety. How can parents discern the real impact of social anxiety and seek help? It starts with objective acceptance.

Chapter 1 of the book started with a questionnaire designed to zero in on the impact of your child's social anxiety. Take a moment to reflect on that questionnaire. Complete it over again if you think things have changed. Your answers are the first step in admitting the problem for your child. As you read through your answers, ask yourself if the negative impact of your child's social anxiety is preventing him or her from participating in school or social events. Is the avoidance easily redirected, or is it difficult? How many events or classes are missed related to social anxiety? Is your child responsive to any of the interventions you've tried? Worksheet #16 reviews these and other questions to ask yourself when trying to determine if the social inhibition rises to the level of concern typical in a case of social anxiety. Use it as a guide to help you decide if you need help with your child.

Where to Find Help

Once you've decided that your child needs professional help, where do you go to find someone? What type of help is best for your child? There are many types of professionals who can assist children with social anxiety, ranging from educators, to pastors and life coaches, to therapists. Deciding what kind of help your child needs involves evaluating the level of severity of anxiety and the impact.

I like to think of interventions as tiers, with Level 1 being the least intrusive, and Level 3 being the most (see Figure 6). Level 1 interventions are easily accessible for the most part and less intensive. They can include education plans developed by school personnel (including the school counselor or psychologist) and the parents that focus on the educational needs of the child. Level 1 interventions may also include the behavioral planning discussed in Chapter 9, as well as any interventions typically done at home. Most of the time, Level 1 interventions will only involve the parent and child, and perhaps an educator.

Worksheet #16

Do We Need Help?

Directions: Take a moment to read and answer each question. Revisit these questions anytime you are concerned about the intensity of your child's social inhibition and avoidance.

1. What is your child currently avoiding?
2. Is your child's anxiety preventing him or her from participating in school and/or social events of interest to the child?
3. How many events or school days have been missed this month related to social avoidance and/or anxiety?
4. What interventions have been attempted? How effective would you consider them?
5. Do you feel your child needs more help at this time?

Take a moment to reflect on your answers. Based on these questions, what are your current concerns? Do you need additional assistance with these concerns?

_____
_____
_____
_____
_____
_____
_____
_____

Intervention Level	Typical Interventions	Intervention Goal
Level 1: General and broad; usually involves an entire class or a schoolwide focus	» Direct teaching of social skills » Set behavior expectations » Direct teaching of social competency skills	» Acquisition of social skills » Compliance with expected behaviors » Development of social competency
Level 2: May be more individualized to a specific student or group of students; focus is still on skill acquisition	» Reteach social skills » Behavior contracts » CBT-like strategies to correct cognition errors	» Acquisition or generalization of social skills » Compliance » Correcting faulty thinking
Level 3: Highly individualized and generally involves serious or intense behaviors	» Behavior contracts » Individualized coaching with mental health professional » Therapy or mental health assistance	» Compliance » Improving social skills use and generalization, building competence, correcting cognition errors » Addressing mental health concerns

Figure 6. Behavior support levels.

Sometimes more intensive interventions are required. Maybe the parents need more specific information with regard to supporting their socially anxious child. Interventions that may be more specifically tailored to the child I consider Level 2. Oftentimes, these interventions will involve the assistance of outside professionals, including a parenting or life coach or a pastoral counselor. These professionals are not mental health professionals, but are often skilled to work with a variety of issues, including low levels of anxiety that do not significantly impact the child's overall mental health, but still require support and/or interventions. Coaches and pastoral counselors can often be found within the community through recommendations from friends and family. Most of the time a disclosure is signed as part of the agreement for services to ensure that you understand that the work you are doing is not considered therapy in any way.

For more intensive treatment, Level 3, you will want to enlist the help of a licensed therapist. This can include clinical social workers, psychologists, licensed counselors, and psychiatrists. All of these types of therapists will usually work with anxiety disorders in a variety of ways. Many insurance policies do cover therapy, so a call to your insurance company may be the best place to start when looking for a licensed mental health professional. As with coaches and pastoral counselors, word of mouth is also a great way to find a therapist.

Regardless of how you find the therapist, it is important to interview the professional to make certain you have a good working relationship. Tip Sheet #29 highlights many of the things you'll want to consider as you find your therapist.

No matter which way you decide to go, with parent coaching, therapy, or a combination of the two, it's important to maintain an open relationship with the professionals you've enlisted to help. Share openly with them, try out the suggestions with an open mind, and keep track of the results. Most of the time there is no quick fix for social anxiety problems. Any intervention process will take time. Often, things may get worse before they get better. As mentioned throughout the book, anxiety responses are easily habituated and often difficult to reshape—difficult, but not impossible. Things do get better. There is hope.

Treatments That Work

Part of the reason I am ultimately very optimistic about improving outcomes for socially anxious children is due to the large amount of research regarding treatment for anxiety disorders. That research has informed therapists and coaches alike on the types of interventions shown to be the most effective with social anxiety, including exposure (desensitization techniques), cognitive training, social skills training including generalization techniques, and relaxation techniques. These strategies are best learned in a therapeutic setting, although the principles can be adapted for use within coaching and educational settings.

Tip Sheet #29

Finding a Therapist

- Get referrals from friends dealing with similar issues or from another trusted professional.
- Interview the professional—ask about his or her knowledge in working with children with SAD, as well as any other issues you believe to be relevant (i.e. giftedness, previous history of trauma, your anxiety, etc).
- Ask for periodic updates regarding your child.
- Trust your instincts—if something feels off for you and your child, it may not be a good fit between you and the professional.
- Remember, things often get worse before they get better. Don't expect a quick fix for your child.

Exposure Techniques

Most therapies specifically designed for the treatment of social anxiety start with some form of exposure therapy. Considered the foundation of any successful behavioral and cognitive-behavioral intervention program, exposure is the process of systematically exposing the child to the source of the anxiety in gradual progression while also engaging in an incompatible behavior like relaxation techniques (Kim, Parr, & Alfano, 2011; Vannest, Reynolds, & Kamphaus, 2008). This strategy is sometimes referred to as systematic desensitization and can be done by imagining the anxiety-producing event or can be used in real-life situations. Typical behaviors incompatible with anxiety include muscle relaxation training, deep breathing exercises, and similar interventions.

I've used many derivatives of exposure therapy with the students I've worked with, often starting by establishing a baseline (the point of exposure to the anxiety-producing stimuli in which the student can continue to function well) and slowly increasing exposure while coaching the child through relaxation exercises. The success rate with this process has always been high for me, as long as the specific steps are not rushed. Tip Sheet #30 includes a basic process for implementing exposure-based techniques and highlights the need to establish a hierarchy of anxiety before starting this type of strategy.

Tip Sheet #30

Systematic Desensitization or Exposure

Directions: Use this tip sheet as a guide to begin to desensitize your child to various situations that elicit strong emotional or anxious reactions. Please note that this should only be done with low-level anxiety-provoking situations unless this is being done in cooperation with a counselor or therapist. When done correctly, this is a powerful way to retrain a child's reaction to stressful stimuli.

- Begin by making a list of the various situations that evoke an anxious response in your child.
- Have your child rank the items on the list from those that bring about the least amount of anxiety, to those that elicit significant anxiety.
- Have the child rate her anxiety on a scale of 0–100 (with 0 being no anxiety and 100 being debilitating anxiety) for each of the events on the list.
- Starting with the situation that causes the least amount of anxiety, break down the task into small steps. If the child is afraid to go to school, for example, start with standing at the door with his or her backpack, then getting in the car, then arriving at school, etc. End with sitting in class.
- Once the steps are laid out, have the child begin to move through each step. With each one, have child rate his or her anxiety at the start of the step. If the anxiety is somewhat high and he or she is unable to try the next step, try a few relaxation exercises to bring the child back to a tolerable level of anxiety.
- Continue moving through the steps in this way until the child is able to successfully get through the entire chain of events.

In addition to establishing a hierarchy for the anxious behavior, it is important for the child to have a working knowledge of how anxiety manifests within his or her body and specific relaxation techniques that produce a desired change in anxiety levels. It is important to note that this technique should only be used with moderately anxious situations for your child unless you are working with a counselor or therapist. It is a very powerful tool and one that can have fantastic results.

Cognitive Training

In addition to exposure therapy, cognitive retraining that focuses on identifying and changing negative self-perceptions is a typical therapeutic approach (Kim et al., 2011). This strategy teaches the child how to identify misperceptions by looking for evidence that contradicts the child's negative point of view. For example, if the child avoids all math tests because she perceives that she will fail the test, be ridiculed in class, and lose friends, cognitive training would focus on finding evidence that the child is actually somewhat successful and that her friends have not laughed or ridiculed her in the past and therefore would not do so in the future.

Another goal of this type of intervention is to help the child refocus from an excessively negative point of view to something more neutral or optimistic. An example of this focus may be the student who has a history of refusing to come to school related to performance anxiety. Using exposure techniques, the child is now attending a few of his classes. However, his negative thinking refuses to allow him to acknowledge the progress as something to celebrate. He sees only what he hasn't yet accomplished. Cognitive training here would help him see the progress as a good thing and refocus his energy on the positive growth instead of the work he still has to accomplish.

Cognitive training is one of the most common approaches used with children. This does not mean it is the most researched option. In truth, the limited research regarding cognitive-based therapies with children suggest that they are not as effective as with adults (Kim et al., 2011). Researchers speculate that this may be due to the lack of negative cognitions with children and young adults, as compared to their adult counterparts. Indeed, it may be that the significant negative thinking trap present in most adult cases of SAD is part of the long-term impact of the disorder and not something that occurs initially (Alfano et al., 2006).

In practical terms, cognitive retraining, while not as crucial with children as with adults, may be a good way to build resiliency, something that can also decrease through long-term engagement in behaviors consistent with social anxiety.

Social Skills Training

As mentioned earlier in this book, social skills deficits are highly correlated with social anxiety (Beidel & Turner, 2007). It is no surprise that a well-rounded intervention plan for SAD should also include some amount of social skills training. This training should be customized to the child's developmental level to allow for similar skills to be taught and to allow for different levels of complexity based on the age-based social expectations at each stage of development.

In addition to structuring the social skills training based on developmental levels, it is important that a training program involve direct teaching as well as a strong focus on generalization to both structured and unstructured settings. Using groups of nonanxious peer helpers in unstructured settings (including everything from pizza parties to playing various games) can enable the child to practice newly acquired social skills in very organic ways without the interference of the therapist or coach. Such opportunities to practice newly acquired skills significantly increase the positive outcomes of this type of intervention (Beidel & Turner, 2007).

Another technique that can work with social skills training is video modeling. The videos can be of other children or the child himself. This type of modeling can be highly effective in reinforcing specific social skills and generalizing a strategy to a new situation. Refer to the social skills tip sheets throughout the book for more information on ways to teach and generalize social skills.

Behavior-Based Techniques

Chapter 9 focused on analyzing behavior and developing plans designed to reshape the behavior away from the nonpreferred behavior and toward a desired outcome. Similar techniques, focusing on contingency management, can have great results in reshaping anxious behaviors (Flood & Wilder, 2004). This strategy focuses on reshaping behavior through the type of behavior planning previously discussed, using reinforcement procedures to change behavior.

Although most clinicians agree that social anxiety is not a conditioned behavior exclusively, it is clearly influenced by basic behavioral conditioning. The parent who responds to the scared child by allowing continual avoidance of the trigger, or the child who is laughed at when he attempts to speak in front of the class is being conditioned to act in a specific way. This conditioning eventually habituates the anxious response. A therapeutic approach that focuses on breaking that conditioning and reshaping the behavior can positively impact the child and reduce the habituated response.

When to Consider Medical Assistance

Sometimes the treatment options previously highlighted are not enough to effect change. This can be particularly true if the child developed SAD at a young age or when comorbid conditions including GAD and depression are evident. In these cases, it may be best to consider medical options.

Medication use with social anxiety is controversial at best. There is limited research regarding the long-term effect of antidepressants and other antianxiety medications with children. This is not to say that use of medication is not recommended. This is a highly personal decision that will need to be made in consultation with your medical doctor. I do think it is important to consult with a pediatric psychiatrist when considering any mental health medications with children. These specialists often understand these medications better than the family doctor or pediatrician.

Whatever your decision regarding medication use, maintaining a behavior journal to indicate any changes in outcome once medications are started can provide the treating doctor with critical information about how your child is responding to the treatment protocol. Similarly, informing the school of changes in medication use is also important.

NONTRADITIONAL APPROACHES TO TREATMENT

There are many therapeutic options for children who suffer with social anxiety. In addition to the traditional methods of exposure, CBT, and social skills training previously discussed, there are additional nontraditional methods beginning to grow in popularity. Although the specific independent research on these methods is unclear, my anecdotal knowledge of these methods from my work with families shows some benefit as a complimentary approach.

Many nontraditional approaches focus on increased relaxation. Yoga, meditation, and message therapy can all benefit children through increased moments of deep relaxation. Also, these practices help create lifelong habits of relaxation that will support reduced levels of anxiety over a lifetime.

Eastern medicine has reported positive results with acupuncture, acupressure, and EFT, or tapping. These strategies involve connecting to the body's natural energy system in order to release anger, frustration, and pain. Practitioners of these interventions report amazing results and quick relief from anxiety-like symptoms (Church, Pina, Reategui, & Brooks, 2012). Similarly, biofeedback focuses on using the body's physical signs to regulate emotion and release pain and anger.

Other nontraditional approaches include art, music, and play therapies. These all use artistic mediums in order to release past pain and anxiety (Epp, 2008).

Deciding whether or not a nontraditional approach is appropriate for you or your child is a highly personal process. As with any treatment option, it is important to research the options for yourself and make an informed decision.

Chalk Talk: Developing Coping Skills Within Your Students

Every educator I speak with wishes for more time to spend educating students. Between working with behavior and anxiety concerns, mediating peer drama, and dealing with a student's lack of independence, many instructional minutes are lost as teachers serve the additional roles of parent, counselor, and coach. Teaching coping strategies on a regular, classwide basis is one way to reduce the negative impact such behaviors can have on instructional time.

Developing strong coping skills does more than teach a kid what to do when he or she is angry. It builds confidence and independence, fosters resiliency, reduces the negative impact of anxiety and other mental health challenges, and promotes safety. And it is easy to do.

Start by dedicating a specific time weekly to practice a skill. The list in Tip Sheet #31 includes many of the typical coping skills that can be easily taught at school. Teach the specific skill, including when to use it. Model the use of the skill and find a way to incorporate positive reinforcement for the skill within your classroom. The more we teach and reinforce positive behaviors, prosocial skills, and coping strategies, the more protective factors our children will develop and the lower the impact of mental health concerns.

MEET SONJI

I met Sonji as a high school senior. He demonstrated significant withdrawal and avoidance during his final years of high school. Although this did not impact his grades significantly, it did impact his ability to interview for both colleges and scholarship opportunities. Sonji's parents asked that I get involved to help him overcome what they referred to as extreme shyness.

SONJI'S STORY

Sonji does not look like someone suffering from anxiety. As his class valedictorian, he has matriculated into a tier I school in the fall. It's hard to believe that 13 months prior, Sonji almost lost the chance to attend his dream school. Anxiety kept Sonji from fulfilling a requirement of the school—an interview.

For as long as Sonji could remember, he hated talking with others. Every time he pictured himself speaking with someone other than his friends, he saw himself tripping over his words, struggling to get out the most simplistic sentence. He imagined the humiliation he'd feel, the way his peers would snicker or laugh, and the look of pity he'd get from his teachers. He was so

Tip Sheet #31

School Coping Skills

Like teaching social skills, teaching children how to cope with adversity is one of the best ways to create safe learning environments and improve student outcomes, especially for children with social anxiety issues. Below is a list of basic coping strategies every student should learn:

- **Develop effective communication skills.** Teach children how to communicate their needs and wants effectively. Strong communication skills are the foundation of any coping skills plan.
- **Establish "safe people" for children to talk to when they are upset.** These people, both on campus and at home, will provide a much-needed sounding board for children wrestling with social anxiety.
- **Teach problem-solving skills.** Understanding how to solve problems is a major life skill. This can involve learning how to understand the problem, recognize social cues, pick an appropriate method of responding, and analyzing results. Understanding what part of the chain your child may struggle with will tell you how best to help. Use behavior journals and Worksheet #12: Understanding My Child's Social Processing (p. 113) to assist in this area.
- **Focus on relaxation.** It is important that children know how to monitor and adjust their emotional states. Knowing which relaxation methods will work best is an important aspect of developing coping strategies.

worried that his fantasies would come true that he managed to manipulate his way out every oral assignment.

Sonji texted instead of making phone calls. He worked in online study groups without video chatting instead of working in groups at school. And he kept himself out of situations that would require him to speak. His teachers knew that Sonji's greatest fear involved speaking, so they required little from him in that regard. After all, Sonji was a genius. What did it matter if he couldn't comfortably present his ideas in verbal form?

Sonji's family didn't worry about their son's withdrawal or avoidance of certain activities. They were confident that he would be able to do what was expected when the time came.

They were wrong.

As Sonji prepared for the college application process, it never occurred to him that he'd have to confront his biggest fears until he was required to be part of a panel interview in order to be eligible for a scholarship at his first choice of school. In addition, the school wanted to interview Sonji as part of his application process.

The idea of sitting with a stranger and conversing sent Sonji into immediate distress. He imagined all of the ways the interview could go wrong. There was no way he could go through with the interview.

Sonji did everything to get out of the interview. He contacted the school and said he was completely unavailable for an interview during the required times. Sonji assumed the school would let him off the hook. Instead they offered a phone interview at a time of his choosing. Sonji panicked.

Sonji's mother came to me requesting help. She knew that I frequently coached kids through similar anxieties and asked me to help her son. My first meeting with Sonji consisted of a somewhat brief interview followed by an exercise in correcting faulty thinking. Sonji's belief about his ability to communicate orally was incorrect and not based in experience or fact. He stated while he never actually experienced a bad interview, he assumed it would happen. Using a chart similar to the one in Worksheet #17, Sonji and I worked to discover and correct his faulty thinking patterns. Soon, Sonji began to see the errors in his thinking.

The next step was addressing his actual fears. Sonji stated that the idea of being embarrassed in front of his peers scared him—no, terrified him. Sonji and I worked on several fear reduction and relaxation exercises similar to those presented throughout the book. Within about 3 months, Sonji was able to participate in interviews. He still didn't feel comfortable in interview-like situations, but he was no longer avoidant of them.

LESSONS LEARNED

Sonji's case isn't like many of the others in the book. In truth, Sonji would likely not meet diagnostic criteria for SAD at all. His anxiety, though a problem, did not inhibit everyday life functioning as it does in typical SAD cases. That said, Sonji's anxiety did present barriers to his ability to obtain his goals. For that reason, I felt like his case was worth examination.

Sonji's case exemplifies the power of situational anxiety to overwhelm anyone's coping system. It also demonstrates the usefulness of several of the book's strategies for a large variety of situations and intensity levels.

Worksheet #17

Is It True?

Directions: Make a list of the internal messages you tell yourself. Then, look for any outside evidence to support or replace the message. Finally, plan out your next steps.

Self-Talk	Truth	New Message or Plan
Example: *I am going to fail at my speech and everyone is going to laugh.*	*No one has laughed before and I am practicing really hard. No one in the class has laughed at the other students.*	*Even though this is scary, I am going to do the best I can. Everyone will appreciate how hard I try.*

Sonji needed a little emotional coaching in order to overcome his fears and correct his faulty thinking. Simple changes in his cognition enabled him to regain control and utilize his coping strategies.

Not every case is this easy. But for Sonji, the time spent correcting his cognition enabled him to move past his fears.

Concluding Thoughts

Finding appropriate help for your socially anxious child isn't always easy. The myriad treatment options and professionals can be difficult to understand and navigate. That said, the overall take-away message regarding treatment should be to diagnose and treat anxieties early. Furthermore, treatment that combines exposure techniques, cognitive retraining, and the teaching of both social skills and coping skills appear to have the best outcomes. Regardless of which one you choose to pursue with your child, it is important to invest the time needed to see a shift in behavior.

It is my hope that this chapter has explained the typical options available to you and your child. More importantly, I sincerely hope that you have found some answers to the questions about shyness and social anxiety that brought you to this book.

If you still have questions, the next section covers some of the frequently asked questions I received in my coaching practice, during parenting classes, and through my social networking sites. If you still have questions in the end, I hope that you will contact me. I am more than willing to help if I can.

PART IV

Social Anxiety FAQs

CHAPTER 11

Social Anxiety 101

Every year, parents ask me how they can support their children in school, overcome anxiety, and improve outcomes for their families. I wanted to share several of the questions related to social anxiety as well as my answers in the hopes that if you've made it to this part of the book and still have questions, you can find what you need here. This chapter deals with basic social anxiety inquires I've received from parents during classes, coaching sessions, and online contacts. I've tried to include practical tip sheets and guides along with my answers.

Q: Do all children with underdeveloped social skills develop some type of social anxiety?

A: Although there does seem to be a relationship between underdeveloped social skills and social anxiety, researchers are unclear as to whether or not a causal relationship exists, and to what extent one causes the other. In my practical experience working with hundreds of children and their families, I can confidently say that not all children with inadequate social skills become socially anxious. I can also confidently say that some children with social anxiety do not demonstrate poor social skills.

Rather than get too hung up on whether or not one will lead to the other, I think it is best to address the specific concerns your child is currently demonstrating. If your child is experiencing a heightened level of social anxiety, focus on strategies that can reduce both the impact of the anxiety and the anxiety itself. Incorporate these strategies as quickly as you can for the best outcomes. Anxiety is easily habituated, so helping the child before behaviors become the primary pattern of responding is very important. I've included several specific strategies throughout the book that may be helpful.

If your child is struggling more with social skill development, focus on incorporating the specific skills he or she seems to be missing into the daily routine. Provide ample opportunities to practice social skills and give performance-based feedback whenever possible. For example, when my child was younger, she loved to talk and often interrupted others with conversations unrelated to the topic currently being discussed. This resulted in negative feedback from her friends, something that bothered her a great deal. Through directly teaching and modeling the desired social skill of listening, helping her resist her impulse to interrupt, and improving her conversation skills, she learned how to better communicate with her friends. Giving her lots of opportunities to practice the skill at home and during playtime solidified the skill for her. Now, she is a strong communicator and no longer receives negative feedback. She can wait her turn, participate in conversations that aren't focused around her, and offer insight into her conversations.

If your child is wrestling with a combination of weak social skill development and social anxiety, it is important to tackle both in tangent. Use the strategies to reduce anxiety while also teaching and reinforcing his or her development of adequate social skills. It will be exhausting work, but worth it.

Q: What would you consider a "normal" amount of social anxiety?

A: Everyone experiences periods of social anxiety—butterflies in your stomach on the first day of school when you meet new friends, tension in your neck when you have to give a speech in class, even a case of mild hives when you start a new school year. These episodes of anxiety happen as you anticipate the upcoming challenge, and fade as soon as the specific event is over. Most of the time, the anxiety isn't repeated the next day you go to school or make a speech. If the stress does return, it is often less than before, as you learned that you can handle the situation and don't *need* to feel afraid. At least, this is the typical response; it is a normal amount of anxiety that ebbs and flows as our skills grow and change.

For some children and adults, however, the anxiety never lessens. It grows and grows. Sometimes this is due to uncomfortable outcomes for the event, such as humiliation and embarrassment. Other times, the anxiety continues because we perceive the outcome as negative, even when it is not. In these cases, the anxiety continues regardless of the outcome. Eventually it becomes entrenched and almost habitual, interfering with "normal" functioning and becoming more of a mental health condition.

It is important to understand that anxiety does happen throughout a lifetime for various reasons. As long as the anxiety is situation specific, lessens with experience and skill development, and does not interfere with daily functioning, it is most likely "normal" and not in need of specialized treatment. If you are ever unsure whether or not you should be concerned about the anxiety you or a family member is experiencing, speak with a therapist just to rule out larger concerns.

Q: How can parents with social anxiety help their children?

A: As I stated in Chapter 3, anxious parents typically raise anxious children. As they seek to protect their children from everything that scares them as parents, their children learn that the world is something to be feared. Their perspective becomes skewed and overly focused on the negative, often resulting in the increased anticipation of danger and the development of anxiety-related symptoms.

To help prevent this endless cycle of fear, it is important that parents with SAD recognize their own fears and anxieties and seek support. Begin to analyze whether or not the things you fear are *actual* threats to your family. If they are not (with socially anxious adults the threat will often be unnecessarily heightened), take the necessary steps to gain control over your own anxieties. Don't hide your struggles or discount your feelings. Socially anxious parents potentially have a lot to offer their children. Learning that anxiety itself is nothing to be feared can be very powerful for a child. Turn your own feelings of shame around and see yourself as a living testament that the impact of social anxiety can be negated. And when those moments happen that overwhelm you, seek help. Set the example to your children that needing support is not a sign of weakness, but a hallmark of both strength and maturity. Worksheet #18 can help you with all of these tasks.

Q. What is the difference between social anxiety and phobias?

A. Phobias are specific irrational and/or excessive fears that result in paralyzing anxiety that adversely impacts daily functioning. These fears can include the fear of leaving your house, the fear of cats, a fear of the number 13, and yes, the fear of social embarrassment resulting from performing in front of others.

Does that last one sound familiar at all? It should. It is the definition of social anxiety. Up until the DSM-5 revision, social anxiety was called social phobia. The change occurred to enable an expansion of the previous definition of social phobia as the fear of performing in front of others to include other fears as well. Social anxiety is now thought of as a fear of any interaction in which the subject is afraid of social embarrassment or humiliation (American Psychiatric Association, 2013b). This can include everything from refusing to go to dinner for fear that you will not be able to maintain a conversation with your relatively unknown date, to the fear of being observed by others because you may be considered abnormal by the observer, to a fear of speaking to your teacher because you don't want to look foolish. All of these situations may elicit an anxious response for the person with social anxiety. Currently, social phobia and social anxiety are used somewhat interchangeably within the research and clinical communities.

Q. Can you outgrow social anxiety?

A. I do not believe that people outgrow social anxiety per se. The term *outgrow* implies a developmental aspect to social anxiety. Although it is true that a child's development can influence the development of

Worksheet #18

The Upside

Directions: If you are wrestling with social anxiety, it is easy to only see the negative aspects of the struggle and feel a sense of shame. But your struggles show children it is possible to wrestle with something difficult and come out a victor! Read the following attributes and decide if it is true for you. Then think of something positive about the attribute or action. Add some of your own attributes and actions. If you are struggling to find anything positive, ask someone to help you. Everything has an upside, even if it is hard to find.

Attribute and/or Action	This Is True for Me (Y/N)	The Positive Side to This
I struggle with social anxiety.		
I often see something as negative when it is not.		
I have to consciously tell myself to be positive.		
I sometimes avoid others.		
Being part of a social event is difficult for me.		

social anxiety in terms of triggering events, there is no research to suggest that people "outgrow" social anxiety.

That said, I have worked with families in which the impact of the anxiety significantly lessens as children mature. As children age, their ability to recognize and change thought patterns typically increase. This can lead to improvements with regard to the management of the anxiety. However, I would not say this is because the child simply grew out of his or her fears. Rather, his or her ability to manage anxiety, as well as his or her ability to recognize and adjust distorted thinking has improved. The improvements likely come as a result of both maturity in thought processes and practice using various cognitive strategies, with the later being the most important of the two.

Interestingly, there is a large body of evidence suggesting that children diagnosed with social anxiety disorder at an early age have a harder time over their life span than those diagnosed in later adolescence or adulthood (Mesa et al., 2011). Although researchers disagree on why this occurs, most concur that those with earlier diagnoses likely have a stronger genetic or biological factor to the anxiety.

Q: What are some strategies for coping with social anxiety for kids and teens?

A: As I've stated throughout the book, anxiety can be paralyzing. Fortunately there are several evidence-based strategies to help, most of them highlighted throughout this book. To make it easier to find specific strategies, I've included a list of some of the best coping strategies for both children and adolescents throughout the book. These strategies are the same ones I've used with a variety of children with good success. The strategies focus on retraining the child's fear response, switching from negative to positive thinking, and learning to discern a "real" threat from a perceived threat. Additionally, some strategies also focus on what to do once the anxiety is already triggered—ways for the child to return to a more balanced state of mind, relax, and move forward.

It is important to know that no specific strategy will work for every child all of the time. As parents and educators, we often "give up" on a specific strategy too soon, assuming that a strategy that is only marginally effective initially won't help the child. I encourage you to use the strategy for at least a few weeks, adjusting it as appropriate for the child and the situation before moving to a new strategy. The last thing you want to do is continually hop from strategy and intervention to strategy and intervention, creating increased anxiety and pulling you and the child away from your goal of improving his or her ability to balance his or her emotions. When a reasonable strategy doesn't work at first, take a deep breath, calm your emotions, and wait. You'll know within a few weeks (and often sooner) whether or not you and your child are moving in the right direction.

Q: What other issues are generally comorbid with this type of anxiety?

A: In Chapter 4, I highlighted a variety of conditions that are typically comorbid with SAD, including depression, separation disorder, other anxiety disorders, and even personality disorders. In children, it is also important to remember that many externalizing behaviors coexist with social anxiety. These can include oppositional behavior, attention problems, and other maladaptive behaviors.

Children, in particular, often express anxiety and fear through a pattern of inappropriate behaviors. Things like impulsively acting out when prompted for work, task and school refusal, and poor peer interactions all can be indicative of not only various behavior disorders, but also symptoms of social anxiety. It is important to always look for the function of the behaviors being exhibited by the child. What is it that the child is trying to get or escape? What is the outcome of the behavior? With a socially anxious child who is afraid of being humiliated, he or she may act out significantly when prompted to complete an oral presentation. This behavior may result in getting sent out of class and being able to skip the oral report, thereby reinforcing the child to again act out whenever he or she wants to avoid a certain type of task.

Now, I'm not saying we should push the child to participate in the oral presentation when his or her anxiety is peaking. But understanding that the behavior is likely more than just willful manipulation will enable those working with the child to help the child ask for a break and return to the task once the anxiety is reduced, drastically improving the outcome for this student.

Q: It seems like there is a strong genetic link to social anxiety. Is there?

A: The research regarding a genetic link to anxiety disorders in general is clear. Study after study has indicated higher rates of SAD among family members. How much of this is related to genetics versus family environment is unclear. But the research does indicate heritability of several traits thought to contribute to the development and diagnosis of SAD, including behavioral inhibition, and fear of negative self-evaluations. The actual connection between those attributes and later evidence of social anxiety still needs to be more thoroughly researched in order to definitely state that there is a clear and profound genetic aspect to social anxiety (Higa-McMillan & Ebesutani, 2011).

My own anecdotal observations with families indicates a combination of both nature and nurture. Many of the children with SAD that I have worked with have one or more parents diagnosed with an anxiety disorder. These parents are often influenced by their own cognitive biases, which shape how they parent and the level of fear present within the daily functioning of the household. It is no suprise to me, then, that their children exhibit similar levels of fear. Whether or not these children would develop social anxiety if the parent did not exhibit his or her own anxious behavior is unknown.

The take-away message regarding genetics, I believe, is that genetics alone do not guarantee the development of SAD. Like most things, developing the disorder requries a combination of predisposing factors, a triggering event (or events), and a consistent pattern of response that habituates that behavior. The complexities of the development of the disorder is part of the reason why SAD can be such a complicated disorder to treat, and why it is important to approach the disorder as wholly as possible.

CHAPTER 12

Social Skills and More
Specific Questions Regarding SAD

In addition to the frequently asked general questions presented in Chapter 11, I do get very specific questions from time to time, dealing with everything from fostering independence, to specific scenarios, to specific populations dealing with social anxiety. The questions below represent a global selection of the questions I've received throughout my practice and for this specific publication. I hope you find the information of use to you as you begin to utilize the various strategies with your socially anxious children.

Q: Should we allow our daughter to use her coping strategies? Or are we fostering a lack of independence by not forcing her to face her fears?

A: This is a very common question I get about weighing the costs and benefits of various intervention strategies. Most parents worry about the negative impact of allowing a child to utilize a specific coping skill as opposed to just pushing through the specific event and "face her fear." Unfortunately, the question itself points to some of the mythology around anxiety disorders as well as other mental health concerns—that these are not "real" problems, but behaviors or feelings we somehow choose. Although it is true that individuals with anxiety can "talk" themselves through the anxiety and learn to lessen or eliminate their response to the fear/threat trigger, it is also true that initially the anxiety is very much out of the individuals' control.

The other problem with this question is the idea that using a coping strategy is somehow indicative of weakness. In truth, all of us use various coping strategies every day. We make to-do lists and program our phones to send reminders for appointments as a way to "cope" with being unable to remember what needs to be accomplished and when. We go for a run, get a drink with friends, or watch mindless TV as a way to "cope" with an overtaxed emotional or nervous system at the end of a hectic and chaotic day. Most of us do not consider any of these very typical coping strategies as indicators of weakness. Coping strategies used by children with anxiety shouldn't be viewed with disdain either.

There are many benefits to the coping strategies recommended throughout this book that go beyond getting through an immediate crisis. Many of the interventions teach bigger life skills that will shape how the child interacts with his or her world throughout a lifetime, enabling the child to participate in his or her life with more confidence. Coping strategies like learning to take a break, balanced lifestyle choices, learning to discern real from perceived threats, and switching from negative to positive mental thinking are all skills that benefit anyone, especially someone with tendencies toward social anxiety.

In getting back to the question, I think coping skills are as important as any other skill we teach our children. Teaching your daughter when to utilize these skills, as well as how to differentiate real from perceived threats can allow her to gain autonomy over her actions, seek her own solutions, and empower her confidence.

Q • Do some people really like parties?
• No, seriously, are there people naturally more gifted at the social game?

A • Absolutely, yes. Some people are more inclined to enjoy the social • milieu of parties. The extroverted child, in particular, will often find the social connections found in a party or group gathering invigorating and as necessary as air, even if he or she doesn't navigate the social dynamics as well as we'd hope.

As for the second part of the question, yes, there are people with naturally stronger social competencies. They are able to navigate the social game with ease, making the rest of us feel somewhat awkward. Fortunately, social skills are learned throughout our lifetime, as we continually grow and refine our social interactions. Most of us will not have a problem developing social skills. We may never enjoy parties, small talk, or other aspects of socialization. But we can still learn adequate skills.

People with social anxiety are different. Not only do they feel awkward around others, they are certain they will face social humiliation within these socially charged environments. This results in avoidance of many social situations and increased gaps in their social skill development. The cycle continues until a true case of social anxiety develops, requiring significant interventions.

The important thing is to catch the early signs of poor social skill development and provide social coaching to your child.

Q: Is social anxiety related to interpersonal relationships, or do other types of nonsocial situations result in social anxiety?

A: As the name implies, social anxiety is related to social events and situations. Interpersonal relationships, typically defined as any social connection or relationship between two or more individuals, is at the heart of social anxiety.

Being related to interpersonal relationships does not mean that social anxiety only happens within the closer, more intimate situations the term *relationship* implies. Social anxiety can develop and be triggered by any social situation in which a person fears being humiliated or embarrassed socially. Sometimes this involves a form of performance akin to performance anxiety. Other times it may relate to being observed or requested to complete work. Any type of situation that could result in social embarrassment has the potential for triggering an anxiety episode within the SAD child.

Q. How can I encourage my anxious and gifted 15-year-old to find friends?

A. Peer relationships can be difficult for any gifted child, regardless of potential anxiety. As discussed in Chapter 1, gifted individuals demonstrate many intensities that resemble anxiety. The combination of these intensities and giftedness can easily result in peer difficulties. Teaching both the social skills related to peer interactions as well as ways to manage intensities is the first and best step to helping any gifted individual in the social arena, usually with very positive outcomes.

Things get a little more complicated for the gifted child who is anxious above and beyond what I would expect with his or her intensities. For this child, it is critical to teach strategies to mitigate the negative mental chatter and replace self-defeating thoughts with positive ones. Cognitive behavioral strategies can be particularly effective for this. Tip Sheet #32 outlines a few specific ways to encourage friendship development in a gifted and anxious child.

It is important to keep temperament in mind when helping any child with friendship development. Some introverted children may not need as much social interaction as a more extroverted child. They may prefer to have a few friends who are very close as opposed to many friends. Forcing the introverted child to have more social involvement than is comfortable is guaranteed to spike an anxious reaction, even in the least apprehensive of people.

Q. Are there family-friendly counseling options when the entire family is introverted and shy?

A. Significant cases of social anxiety are well handled in a therapeutic environment, with counseling that focuses on correcting the distorted thought inherent with SAD. Evidence-based approaches including cognitive behavioral therapy (CBT) and exposure therapy are often utilized by a counselor or therapist to help the person with anxiety replace negative thought patterns and discern between real and perceived threats. When the person with SAD is a child, this therapy may also include the

Tip Sheet #32

Making Friends

- Provide opportunities for your child to meet potential friends and develop/practice social skills. This can include school, activities, church, and other social arenas. Don't be afraid to use social networking tools to help children find others with similar interests. As with any potentially risky tool, however, make sure you are practice safety.
- Teach social skills centered around friendships, including the following
  o introducing yourself,
  o maintaining appropriate boundaries,
  o making good eye contact, and
  o basic conversation skills.

- Keep in mind temperament when arranging playdates.
- Model good friendship habits. Be willing to share your own friendship stories, your successes, as well as your struggles.

parents in order to help generalize the skills learned into the home and school settings.

But what if the family feels too shy or uncomfortable to attend therapy? What if talk therapy is too hard for the introverted child or parent?

You're in luck! CBT and exposure therapies can be done in a variety of ways, including in the counselor's office or at home. Similar strategies are even incorporated into coaching techniques and apps. There is no shortage of ways for the reluctant participant to be able to access these techniques, including self-directed programs, both workbooks and apps, that are based on CBT and exposure therapeutic models.

It's important to note that self-directed programs are not the best option for significant cases of anxiety. When the child is demonstrating significant behaviors like school refusal and selective mutism, it is vital that the family work with a highly trained professional, typically a therapist. Don't let the title scare you; most therapists don't use traditional talk therapy in cases of anxiety. Skilled professionals will be able to work with introverts, shy individuals, and the most reluctant of children in some way. It may take time, but eventually the skilled therapist will be able to forge a therapeutic relationship with the reluctant client.

The therapist also will be able to provide the family with specific interventions to practice at home. The more work that is done outside of the therapist's office, at times when the anxiety is triggered, the more skilled the child and family will become at managing the anxiety and redirecting the self-defeating thought processes.

Q: What are the best CBT options for family-led activities for supporting socially anxious children?

A: CBT is a type of therapy that focuses on correcting errors within our thoughts that result in an anxious or inappropriate response. Evidence-based and highly effective for cases of SAD, most of these therapies involve learning to focus and recognize faulty thinking, as well as learning to replace the self-defeating thoughts with more positive ones. The majority of workbooks, self-directed programs, and apps specifically developed for anxiety problems are rooted in CBT techniques. Worksheet #19 is one example of a very helpful CBT-inspired strategy for building social competency. This, as well as Worksheets #3 (p. 30) and #11 (p. 107), and Questionnaire #7 (p. 140) were all developed using CBT-like techniques.

It is important to note that not all children with SAD will find CBT an effective treatment. In those cases when the CBT exercises do not yield the desired outcome, it is important to consult with a professional for additional assistance. This is particularly true if the person with SAD is developing depression.

Q: It seems like everyone is overly anxious these days. Is social anxiety on the rise, or is it being overidentified?

A: It's no secret that we live in a stressful world. Longer work days, increased noise from our interconnectedness, and decreases in healthy habits to balance out the demands have all resulted in increased

Worksheet #19

Developing Social Competence

Directions: The majority of the worksheets and self-reflection tools in this book have their root in cognitive behavioral therapy (CBT). In particular, Worksheets #3 (p. 30) and #4 (p. 42) are particularly helpful at correcting cognitive biases.

This worksheet is one of my favorites to use with parents and children. The directions are simple—complete the worksheet as indicated, trying out different solutions in the book, and reflecting on the outcomes. Determine which solutions work best for you and your children.

Skill	Potential Obstacles	Solutions
Conversation skills	*Example: Initiating a conversation with someone I barely know*	*Practice at home using a script.*
Relaxation		
Flexibility		
Inner stillness		
Humor		

SAD Symptoms

Physical
- » Nausea
- » Headaches
- » Sweating palms
- » Racing heart

Emotional
- » Fear of embarrassment or humiliation
- » Fear of being called on in class
- » Fear of being watched or judged
- » Performance-based fears
- » Heightened threat perception

Behaviors
- » Avoiding social gatherings and events
- » Avoiding performance opportunities in class
- » Attendance problems
- » Constant negative thinking

Figure 7. Social anxiety disorder symptoms.

stress and anxiety. We expect more social connection from individuals, less "down time," and higher levels of performance. We can't be surprised that more and more people are demonstrating periods of anxiety. It's important, however, not to confuse this situation-specific stress and anxiety with the diagnosed condition of social anxiety disorder.

For the majority of us, periods of increased stress and anxiety will wax and wane throughout our lifetime. It may even be strong enough to disrupt daily functioning for a day or two. In these cases, we adjust, utilize our skill set to correct faulty thinking, reduce our stress, and push through our fears. This is not social anxiety.

The person with SAD will not be able to push forward. For him or her, the impact of the anxiety-provoking event will be cumulative, building until a true case of social anxiety disorder is formed.

To get back to the question, no. Social anxiety is not being overidentified, I think. Rather, we are using the term somewhat indiscriminately, including cases of situational stress within our conversations of social anxiety. Take a look at the list of the criteria for a diagnosis of SAD again (see Figure 7). It is clear that this is more than a simple case of too much stress.

CHAPTER 13

Educators Ask Questions

I have received many questions about social anxiety over the years from parents. But the majority of questions I get on a daily basis come from educators. Here is a short list of the typical types of questions and biases that come up whenever I am speaking with educators.

Q. **How can I tell if one of my students has social anxiety and what should I do?**

A. This book highlights the basic symptoms and warning signs for anxiety. To make it easy for educators, I thought I'd make a "Quick Facts About Social Anxiety Disorder" sheet for use in the classroom (see Tip Sheet #33). This sheet can be put into a teacher's reference notebook or adapted as needed. It provides the symptoms and hallmarks of social anxiety, along with a basic guide for interventions. It is important to note that this sheet is not meant as a replacement for this book. It's only a quick reference guide meant to be used after you've gained a good base of knowledge about social anxiety and general tips for interventions.

Q. **How do I know when to push my students to participate in class and when I should just back off?**

A. Achieving a balance between pushing students to reach their potential and shielding them from becoming too overwhelmed is

Tip Sheet #33

Quick Facts About
Social Anxiety Disorder

Symptoms:
- Fear of being called on in class
- Fear of being watched or judged
- Expressions of nausea or headaches in reaction to being called on in class or other performance demands
- Avoiding social gatherings
- Avoiding social situations
- Avoiding performance opportunities in class
- Attendance problems

Triggers:
- Being called on in class
- A new school or classroom
- Performance demands
- New social situations

What you can do:
- Create a safe and nurturing environment
- Create safe zones on campus for the student
- Utilize break cards as necessary for planned "stress" breaks
- Teach relaxation strategies
- Focus on correcting faulty thinking patterns

a difficult thing to navigate. This is especially true if you are working with a student or students with social anxiety disorder. These students will react differently to the demands in the classroom, both in social and academic domains. Some may be triggered by group projects or oral presentations. Others may have little difficulties with that type of expectation, but struggle with the teacher walking around to "check" their work or with peer editing.

It is important to understand each of your students as individuals to be able to know how much "pushing" they can handle. Use the first few weeks of school to not only assess their academic levels and learning differences, but spend time watching how they react in group settings or during whiteboard and similar activities. Can your students function within a Socratic seminar format or when presented with a pop quiz? How are they on the campus during unstructured times or during electives and P.E.? All of this information will tell you which students are introverts and which are extroverts; it will tell you who thrives on challenges and who shrinks from them. And it will begin to inform you of what each of your students are prepared to handle in terms of pressure.

Yes, your students will change throughout the school year. So be prepared to monitor and adjust your expectations and how your students demonstrate growth. Likewise, if your students begin to struggle or show signs of distress, be ready to adjust the workload demands until relief is achieved. No one learns under duress. It is important that a culture of caring be carefully cultivated in your classroom and the school. Tip Sheet #34 recaps some basic warning signs that a student may be struggling emotionally. This quick reference guide does not speak to the cause of the distress, only that a student's emotional needs may be elevating and can potentially impact his or her functional levels in your classroom.

Q: I worry about my students faking social anxiety just to get out of work. Is there a way to tell if they are "faking"?

A: This is a typical question I get from teachers, and one that bothers me in a lot of ways. The idea that we, as educators, need to be "on guard" for students whose goal is to manipulate the system to get out of work is not one I want educators to latch on to. And yet, I do not live in a bubble. I know that there are students who have manipulated their way out of situations in the past; that is why there is a sensitivity to it now. But, I don't believe in addressing this concern with assumptions. In fact, I think that even the student caught manipulating the teacher is asking for help in some way.

I think the best way to approach all children is to assume that the concern, any concern, is real. This is not to say that the reason for the concern, or the label we've placed on the behavior, is accurate. But as

Tip Sheet #34

Emotional Distress Warning Signs: A Guide for Educators

Everyone feels stress from time to time. However, sometimes the signs of stress may be an indicator of a more serious problem. Here is a list of some of the warning signs in school-aged children that there may be a more significant emotional issue going on:

- Extreme hyperactivity compared to peers
- Extreme worrying or crying compared to peers
- Increases in tantrum and aggressive behaviors
- A sudden change in performance
- Loss of interest in school or social activities
- Changes in attendance
- Sudden change in appearance
- Excessive concern regarding weight
- Sudden change in friendships
- Sudden or increased withdrawal
- Expressing a desire to harm self or others

I mentioned earlier, all maladjusted behavior, whether the source is a mental illness, intensities of some form, or a manipulation, are cause for us to support the child and teach him or her a different way of acting to get his or her needs met. This may include taking the parent and child at their word initially. Support the anxiety problem if that is what the parents and/or child has indicated is the problem. If the problem turns out to be manipulation, then address that. You will have caused no harm in providing extra supports for the child who is "faking it." On the other hand, you may cripple a child who you *believe* to be faking but who is actually experiencing severe trauma.

Bottom line, if a parent believes a child needs support, if a child acts in a way suggesting the need for support, then we, as educators, need to find ways to support that child and family. It is what's best for kids, best for our communities, and ultimately best for our schools and achievement. Whatever the reason for the support, what if we just worried more about supporting the child than possibly allowing a manipulation to occur? I'm willing to bet we'd all sleep better if we just focused on supporting children.

Q: Won't many of my students use the social anxiety label to get out of oral presentations of group assignments?

A: This question comes from a similar place as the one above, and another question that speaks to our fear as educators—that we aren't doing our job when children "get out" of tasks. Although I absolutely believe that all children need to learn to speak orally and meet the standards to the best of their ability level, I also believe there are a million ways to get from point A to point B, and we don't need to all arrive at the same point in the same way. We are diverse as human beings. Our education should be somewhat diverse as well. That said, it is hard to differentiate for all children.

In the specific case of this question, I think the answer depends on why the student is trying to avoid the presentation, and where that student is in his or her skill development related to the social anxiety. As discussed throughout the book, social anxiety can affect children in a variety of ways. Some are hindered during oral presentations, while others are not. It is important to understand the way social anxiety impacts your specific student. If he or she is experiencing significant anxiety during oral presentations, find a way to take baby steps. Have the student present to a friend or to you initially. If that is still too difficult, utilize technology and try having the student create a vlog or podcast to present to you at first, and maybe to the class later. Teach him or her to take a break and do a few relaxation or mental preparation exercises prior to the presentation. Teach the class how to respond to presentations in an appropriate way to ensure a caring environment. All of these things will help move your student forward, while continuing to honor the difficulties he or she may be facing.

Learning to overcome fears is an important task for the socially anxious. And while we, as educators, can help facilitate that task by stretching our students beyond what they think they can do, it is important to provide a safety net as they learn to overcome their obstacles.

Q: Kids really aren't supposed to socialize in my classroom, so why do I need to worry about social anxiety?

A: One of the more common myths I correct regarding social anxiety is that this is about making friends or interacting with peers. Yes, some students with SAD do struggle in these areas. But it is a fear of social embarrassment or humiliation that drives social anxiety. This can happen in a class environment when a student asks a question, or during a presentation, or even when a child gets sick during a test. All of these scenarios are potential triggers for social anxiety. Knowing the warning signs, and more importantly, how to intercede effectively, can help you create a socially safe environment for all learners.

As mentioned in the opening of the book, SAD is one of the most prevalent anxiety disorders, affecting approximately 9%–12% of the population. That can mean 3–4 students per class or more. Given that statistic, every educator needs to be informed about the symptoms and what to do to help.

Q: Does SAD prevent a student from spontaneously engaging in conversation?

A: The answer is a definitive maybe. I know—not the best answer, right? But the truth is that most of the time SAD will inhibit a person's ability to socially engage, including through spontaneous conversation. Most of the time, but not all of the time. Some people with SAD can engage when the conversation is not focused on performance (like sports and academics). In these moments, the person with social anxiety does not demonstrate his or her symptoms. It is as though there is no anxiety at all. However, once that same person is asked to participate in a Socratic-style seminar, for example, he or she may fall completely mute, unable to articulate any ideas. It may even appear as though that student didn't read any of the material for the class and therefore has nothing to say. This is far from true. Odds are that same student was well prepared but inhibited from responding related to his or her social anxiety.

There are several things that you can do to help the student who falls into this category. First, prepare the child for the expectations and remind him or her of coping strategies prior to the actual task. In this way, the student is not caught off guard and can utilize a strategy to calm him or herself before shutting down completely.

Q: If social anxiety develops as a result of both heredity and environmental shaping, will the siblings of a student with SAD also shows signs of anxiety?

A: As educators, we often work with many siblings within a family, something that is good and potentially hard. I like this question as it speaks to the nature versus nurture aspect of social anxiety. As discussed in earlier chapters, social anxiety develops as a result of hardwiring and genetics, coupled with environmental conditioning and triggering events. Although there is some research that says anxious parents and anxious households are significantly more likely to produce anxious children, I think it is important that each case be looked at separately. Yes, there is a likelihood that siblings may share features of social anxiety, as the question states. But it is not a guarantee. There are several other factors to consider, including the unique nature of the child's social experiences, resiliency levels, and other types of hardwiring, including cognition and temperament. Each student who comes into our room has to be taken on his or her own unique merit.

Which brings me to another point—it is very important that we don't assume behavior about our students prior to working with them. Meaning, try to not predetermine a student's abilities, behaviors, and potential based on their school records or what your colleagues say over lunch. People do change. The student who struggled in one class with one teacher may not function that way for you. Yes, past history can inform the present. If a child has been identified as having exceptional needs, it is important to understand and support those needs as soon as possible. Equally important, however, is our willingness to accept that the student may grow and change.

Q: I have a student identified as having SAD, but he functions fine in my class. Does he really have the disorder, or is he more likely misidentified?

A: A common theme throughout the book has been about the unique nature of SAD and the ability for the symptoms to both ebb and flow over time and change based on environment. It is possible that a child with SAD does not feel threatened in your classroom, and therefore is not consistently manifesting the behaviors associated with social anxiety. That is not to say he was misidentified. More likely, the current environment so appropriately meets the student's needs that he or she is not being triggered.

In this scenario, it is important that the naturally occurring supports in your classroom environment be recognized and notated in some way. This can help ensure that future teachers are able to get similar results with the student, while simultaneously understanding the specific types of interventions that work for the student. Both pieces of information can secure positive outcomes for the school and the student in the future.

Q: What are some examples of things I can do to support my children with anxiety while also holding them to the high standards I expect from all of my students?

A: Another myth about supporting the unique needs of students is that doing so somehow negates the high standards we hold for all students. Nothing could be further from the truth. Offering a supportive environment refers to specific accommodations to learning styles or social/behavioral/emotional considerations. It does not refer to mastery expectations. Put another way, accommodations for unique learners refers to changing *how* we get the information to the student and/or from the student, not *what* overall content we expect.

Imagine a student with social anxiety that inhibits his participation in group peer-editing activities. Your assignment has groups of four exchange papers and read/edit them, then share within the group. This causes significant emotional upheaval for your anxious student, often causing him to miss school on editing days. One accommodation could be to have his group be two people instead of four. Perhaps the edits are not shared in an oral fashion, but in writing—something he can review after school. These simple changes to how he demonstrates mastery aren't asking you to reduce your expectations, just change how he demonstrates the task.

The key to utilizing similar accommodations is to take time to know the child and his or her unique needs. Then analyze the tasks to know the ways they can be accommodated. Use some of the suggestions in this book, as well as suggestions from colleagues, the school psychologist or school counselor, and an administrator. It can seem like a lot of work initially, but once you discover the simple adjustments that work for your student, you can replicate results with ease.

Final Thoughts

Children with social anxiety hold a dear place in my heart. Their world is often filled with feelings of apprehension and fear. They look for threats around every social corner and often picture embarrassment and humiliation every time they leave their homes.

Raising children who struggle in this way can be a challenge. Maybe you can't understand what is happening with your child and why they just don't push through the fear. Perhaps you were an anxious child and you're being triggered as you watch your child's struggles. Or perhaps you just feel at a loss, overwhelmed with the task of teaching him or her how to move past the anxiety and apprehension.

It's my hope that the information and evidence-based strategies provided throughout the book will give you hope and understanding, a fresh view into the world of an anxious child. You may even have more insight into yourself or your spouse.

There are many tips, questionnaires, and strategies presented throughout the book. At first glance, they no doubt appear easy. Rooted in a common sense approach, these strategies are deliberately worded in simple terms to make them accessible during moments of crisis. Please do not assume that they are too simple, too mundane to work. Each strategy and intervention was developed using research-based approaches known to effectively work with social anxiety. The interventions have been well accepted in the literature as being effective when performed consistently.

And therein lies the difficulty.

These skills need to be practiced and adjusted to meet the needs of you and your family. Not every strategy will work for every person. Find the ones that work best for you and start there. But make sure you are well grounded in the informational part of the book first. This will give you the foundation you need to truly understand the nature of what is happening with your child.

You may come to a time when you feel like you've failed your child, a time when you think you were ineffective in parenting and "hurt" your child. As long as you are trying, as long as you are invested in doing the best you can and helping your child in the best way you can, you have not failed, no matter how it may feel at times.

Learning to be an effective parent takes times. You will make mistakes (notice I said mistakes, not failure). Just stay focused on helping your child develop the skills necessary to rise from his or her anxiety and move past his or her fear.

SAD does not have to be a paralyzing illness. Your child can develop the skills to live a life free from fear. Your child can develop his or her own ways of reducing anxiety and building resiliency. When this happens, celebrate! It is a well-deserved victory for all of you.

I would love to hear from you and your family about this journey. Contact me with your own stories and suggestions. I can be reached via e-mail at Christine@christinefonseca.com or on my many social networking sites. Together we can help our children move beyond their inhibition and anxiety.

References

Affrunti, N. W., & Woodruff-Borden, J. (2014). Parental perfectionism and overcontrol: Examining mechanisms in the development of child anxiety. *Journal of Abnormal Child Psychology*, 1–13. doi:10.1007/s10802-014-9914-5

Alfano, C. A., & Beidel, D. C. (2011). Introduction. In C. A. Alfano & D. C. Beidel (Eds.), *Social anxiety in adolescents and young adults: Translating developmental science into practice* (pp. 3–8). Washington, DC: American Psychological Association.

Alfano, C. A., Beidel, D. C., & Turner, S. M. (2006). Cognitive correlates of social phobia among children and adolescents. *Journal of Abnormal Child Psychology, 34,* 189–201. doi:10.1007/s10802-005-9012-9

American Psychiatric Association. (2013a). *Diagnostic and statistical manual of mental disorders* (5th ed.). Arlington, VA: American Psychiatric Publishing.

American Psychiatric Association. (2013b). *Social anxiety.* Retrieved from http://www.dsm5.org/Documents/Social%20Anxiety%20Disorder%20Fact%20Sheet.pdf

Barlow, D. H. (2004). *Anxiety and its disorders: The nature and treatment of anxiety and panic* (2nd ed.). New York, NY: Guilford Press.

Beidel, D. C., & Turner, S. M. (2007). *Shy children, phobic adults: Nature and treatment of social anxiety disorder* (2nd ed.). Washington, DC: American Psychological Association.

Beidel, D. C., Turner, S. M., & Dancu, C. (1985). Physiological, cognitive, and behavioral aspects of social anxiety. *Behaviour Research and Therapy, 23,* 109–117. doi:10.1016/0005-7967(85)90019-1

Benoit, D. (2004). Infant-parent attachment: Definition, types, antecedents, measurement and outcome. *Paediatrics & Child Health, 9,* 541–

545. Retrieved from http://www.ncbi.nlm.nih.gov/pmc/articles/ PMC2724160/

Bernstein, B. E. (2014). *Social phobia*. Retrieved from http://emedicine. medscape.com/article/290854-overview

Biggs, B. K., Sampilo, M. L., & McFadden, M. M. (2011). Peer relations and victimization in adolescents with social anxiety disorder. In C. A. Alfano & D. C. Beidel (Eds.), *Social anxiety in adolescents and young adults: Translating developmental science into practice* (pp. 143–160). Washington, DC: American Psychological Association.

Bogels, S. M., Alden, L., Beidel, D. C., Clark, L. A., Pine, D. S., Stein, M. B., & Voncken, M. (2010). Social anxiety disorder: Questions and answers for the DSM-V. *Depression and Anxiety, 27,* 168–189.

Bogels, S. M., van Oosten, A., Muris, P., & Smulders, D. (2001). Familial correlates of social anxiety in children and adolescents. *Behaviour Research and Therapy, 39,* 273–287. doi:10.1016/S0005-7967(00)00005-X

Bohlin, G., Hagekull, B., & Rydell, A. (2000). Attachment and social functioning: A longitudinal study from infancy to middle childhood. *Social Development, 9,* 24–39. doi:10.1111/1467-9507.00109

Broeren, S., Newall, C., Dodd, H. F., Locker, R., & Hudson, J. L. (2014). Longitudinal investigation of the role of temperament and stressful life events in childhood anxiety. *Development and Psychopathology, 26,* 437–449. doi:10.1017/S0954579413000989

Brühl, A. B., Delsignore, A., Komossa, K., & Weidt, S. (2014). Neuroimaging in social anxiety disorder—A meta-analytic review resulting in a new neurofunctional model. *Neuroscience & Biobehavioral Reviews, 47,* 260–280. doi:10.1016/j.neubiorev.2014.08.003

Campione-Barr, N., Greer, K. B., & Kruse, A. (2013). Differential associations between domains of sibling conflict and adolescent emotional adjustment. *Child Development, 84,* 938–954. doi:10.111/cdev.12022

Cartwright-Hatton, S., Tschernitz, N., & Gomersall, H. (2005). Social anxiety in children: social skills deficit or cognitive distortion? *Behaviour Research and Therapy, 43,* 131–141. Retrieved from http://web.monroecc.edu/manila/webfiles/cfinch/socialanxiety1.pdf

Chua, A. (2011). *The battle hymn of the tiger mother.* New York, NY: Penguin Press.

Church, D., Pina, O., Reategui, C., & Brooks, A. (2012). Single-session reduction of the intensity of traumatic memories in abused adolescents after EFT: A randomized controlled pilot study. *Traumatology: An International Journal, 18*(3), 73–79. doi:10.1177/153476561 1426788

Conti-Ramsden, G., & Botting, N. (2004). Social difficulties and victimization in children with SLI at 11 years of age. *Journal of Speech, Language and Hearing Research, 47,* 145–161. doi:10. 1044/1092-4388(2004/013)

Crick, N. R., & Dodge, K. A. (1994). A review and reformulation of social information-processing mechanisms in children's social adjustment. *Psychological Bulletin, 115,* 74–101. doi:10.1037/0033-2909.115.7.74

D'Augelli, A. R., Grossman, A. H., & Starks, M. T. (2008). Families of gay, lesbian, and bisexual youth: What do parents and siblings know and how do they react? *Journal of GLBT Family Studies, 4,* 95–115.

Epp, K. M. (2008). Outcome-based evaluation of a social skills program using art therapy and group therapy for children on the autism spectrum. *Children & Schools, 30*(1), 27–36. doi:10.1093/cs/30.1.27

Erath, S. A., Flanagan, K. S., & Bierman, K. L. (2007). Social anxiety and peer relations in early adolescence: Behavioral and cognitive factors. *Journal of Abnormal Child Psychology, 35,* 405–416. doi:10.1007/s10802-007-9099-2

Freitas-Ferrari, M. C., Hallak, J. E., Trzesniak, C., Machado-de-Sousa, J. P., Chagas, M. H. N., Nardi, A. E., & Crippa, J. A. S. (2010). Neuroimaging in social anxiety disorder: a systematic review of the literature. *Progress in Neuro-Psychopharmacology and Biological Psychiatry, 34,* 565–580.

Flood, W. A., & Wilder, D. A. (2004). The use of differential reinforcement and fading to increase time away from a caregiver in a child with speration anxiety disorder. *Education and Treatment of Children, 27*(1), 1–8. Retrieved from http://www.freepatentsonline.com/article/Education-Treatment-Children/115503120.html

Fonseca, C. (2011). *Emotional intensity in gifted students: Helping kids cope with explosive feelings.* Waco, TX: Prufrock Press.

Fonseca, C. (2014). *Quiet kids: Help your introverted child succeed in an extroverted world.* Waco, TX: Prufrock Press.

Fox, N. A., Henderson, H. A., Marshall, P. J., Nichols, K. E., & Ghera, M. M. (2005). Behavior inhibition: Linking biology and behavior within a developmental framework. *Annual Review of Psychology, 56,* 235–262. doi:10.1146/annurev.psych.55.090902.141532

Fujiki, M., Brinton, B., Isaacson, T., & Summers, C. (2001). Social behaviors of children with language impairment on the playground: A pilot study. *Language, Speech, and Hearing Services in Schools, 32,* 101–113. doi:10.1044-0161-1461(2001/008)

Hariri, A. R., Mattay, V. S., Tessitore, A., Fera, F., & Weinberger, D. R. (2003). Neocortical modulation of the amygdala response to fearful stimuli. *Biological Psychiatry, 53,* 494–501. doi:10.1016/S0006-3223(02)01786-9

Hart, K. I., Fujiki, M., Brinton, B., & Hart, C. H. (2004). The relationship between social behavior and severity of language impairment. *Journal of Speech, Language, and Hearing Research, 47,* 647–662. doi:10.1044/1092-4388(2004-050)

Hébert, T. P. (2011). *Understanding the social and emotional lives of gifted students.* Waco, TX: Prufrock Press.

Heiser, N. A., Turner, S. M., & Beidel, D. C. (2003). Shyness: Relationship to social phobia and other psychiatric disorders. *Behaviour Research and Therapy, 41,* 209–221. doi:10.1016/S0005-7967(02)00003-7

Heitmann, C. Y., Peterburs, J., Mothes-Lasch, M., Hallfarth, M. C., Böhme, S., Miltner, W. H., & Straube, T. (2014). Neural correlates of anticipation and processing of performance feedback in social anxiety. *Human brain mapping, 35,* 6023–6031. doi:10.1002/hbm.22602

Henderson, L., & Zimbardo, P. (1998). Shyness. In *Encyclopedia of mental health* (Vol. 3, pp. 497–509). San Diego, CA: Academic Press.

Higa-McMillan, C. K., & Ebesutani, C. (2011). The etiology of social anxiety disorder in adolescents and young adults. In C. A. Alfano & D. C. Beidel (Eds.), *Social anxiety in adolescents and young adults: Translating developmental science into practice* (pp. 29–51). Washington, DC: American Psychological Association.

Holly, L. E., & Pina, A. A. (2014). Variations in the influence of parental socialization of anxiety among clinic referred children. *Child Psychiatry & Human Development, 1*–11. doi:10.1007/s10578-014-0487-x

Individuals with Disabilities Education Improvement Act, Pub. Law 108-446 (December 3, 2004).

Jung, C. G. (1971). *Psychological types: The collected works of C.G. Jung, Vol. 6* (R. F. Hull, Ed., & H. G. Baynes, Trans.). Princeton, NJ: Princeton University Press.

Kagan, J. (1989). Temperamental contributions to social behavior. *American Psychologist, 44,* 668–674. doi:10.1037/0003-066X.44.4.668

Kashdan, T. B., & Herbert, J. D. (2001). Social anxiety disorder in childhood and adolescence: Current status and future directions. *Clinical Child and Family Psychology Review, 4,* 37–61. doi:10.1023/A:1009576610507

Kearney, C. A., Gauger, M., Schafer, R., & Day, T. (2011). Social and performance anxiety and oppositional and school refusal behavior in adolescents. In C. A. Alfano & D. C. Beidel (Eds.), *Social anxiety in adolescents and young adults: Translating developmental science into practice* (pp. 125–141). Washington, DC: American Psychological Association.

Kessler, R. C., Stang, P., Wittchen, H. U., Stein, M., & Walters, E. E. (1999). Lifetime comorbidities between social phobia and mood disorders in the U.S. National Comorbidity Survey. *Psychological Medicine, 29,* 555–567. doi:10.1017/S0033291799008375

Kidron, Y., & Fleischman, S. (2006). Promoting adolescents' prosocial behavior. *Educational Leadership, 63*(7), 90–91. Retrieved from http://www.broward.k12.fl.us/k12programs/MiddleSchools/Reference%20Library_files/PROMOTING%20PROSOCIAL%20BEHAVIOR.pdf

Kim, K. L., Parr, A. F., & Alfano, C. A. (2011). Behavioral and cognitive behavioral treatments for social anxiety disorder in adolescents and young adults. In C. A. Alfano & D. C. Beidel (Eds.), *Social anxiety in adolescents and young adults: Translating developmental science into practice* (pp. 245–264). Washington, DC: American Psychological Association.

Kostelnik, M., Gregory, K., Soderman, A., & Whiren, A. (2012). *Guiding children's social development and learning (What's new in early childhood)* (7th ed.). Belmont, CA: Wadsworth.

La Greca, A., Davila, J., Landoll, R. R., & Siegel, R. (2011). Dating, romantic relationships, and social anxiety in young people. In C. A. Alfano & D. C. Beidel (Eds.), *Social anxiety in adolescents and young adults: Translating developmental science into practice* (pp. 93–105). Washington, DC: American Psychological Association.

Laney, M. O. (2002). *The introvert advantage: How to thrive in an extrovert world.* New York, NY: Workman Publishing.

Lang, P. (1968). Fear reduction and fear behavior: Problems in treating a construct. In J. M. Schlien (Ed.), *Research in psychotherapy* (Vol. 3, pp. 90–102). Washington, DC: American Psychological Association.

Lieb, R., Wittchen, H., Hofler, M., Fuetsch, M., Stein, M., & Merikangas, K. (2000). Parental psychopathology, parenting styles, and the risk of social phobia in offspring: A prospective-longitudinal community study. *Archives of General Psychiatry, 57,* 859–866. doi:10.1001/archpsyc.57.9.859

Magee, W. J. (1999). Effects of negative life experiences on phobia onset. *Social Psychiatry and Psychiatric Epidemiology, 34,* 343–351. doi:10.1007/s001270050154

Mesa, F., Nieves, M. M., & Beidel, D. C. (2011). Clinical presentation of social anxiety disorder in asolescents and young adults. In C. A. Alfano & D. C. Beidel (Eds.), *Social anxiety in adolescents and young adults: Translating developmental science into practice* (pp. 11–28). Washington, DC: American Psychological Association.

Metzler, C. W., Biglan, A., Rusby, J. C., & Sprague, J. R. (2001). Evaluation of a comprehensive behavior management program to improve school-wide positive behavior support. *Education and Treatment of Children, 24,* 448–479.

Miers, A. C., Blote, A. W., Bogels, S. M., & Westenberg, P. M. (2008). Interpretation bias and social anxiety in adolescents. *Journal of Anxiety Disorders, 22,* 1462–1471. doi:10.1016/j.janxdis.2008.02.010

Muris, P., Meesters, C., Merckelbach, H., & Hulsenbeck, P. (2000). Worry in children is related to perceived parental rearing and attachment. *Behaviour Research and Therapy, 38,* 487–497. doi:10.1016/S0005-7967(99)00072-8

National Center for Education Statistics. (2013). *Student reports of bullying and cyber-bullying: Results from the 2011 school crime supplement to the national crime victimization survey.* Retrieved from http://nces.ed.gov/pubs2013/2013329.pdf

Phillips, M. L., Drevets, W., Rauch, S., & Lane, R. (2003). Neurobiology of emotion perception I: The neural basis of normal emotion perception. *Biological Psychiatry, 54,* 504–514. doi:10.1016/S0006-3223(03)00168-9

Probst, B. (2007, January/February). When your child's exceptionality is emotional: Looking beyond psychoiatric diagnosis. *Twice Exceptional Newsletter.* Retrieved from http://www.sengifted.org/archives/articles/when-your-childs-exceptionality-is-emotional-looking-beyond-psychiatric-diagnosis

Rapee, R. M. (2014). Preschool environment and temperament as predictors of social and nonsocial anxiety disorders in middle adolescence. *Journal of the American Academy of Child & Adolescent Psychiatry, 53,* 320–328. doi:10.1016/j.jaac.2013.11.014

Richards, T. A. (2014). *What is social anxiety?* Retrieved from https://socialanxietyinstitute.org/what-is-social-anxiety

Roberts, K. E., Schwartz, D., & Hart, T. A. (2011). Social anxiety among lesbian, gay, bisexual, and transgender adolescents and young adults. In C. A. Alfano & D. C. Beidel (Eds.), *Social anxiety in adolescents and young adults: Translating developmental science into practice* (pp. 161–181). Washington, DC: American Psychological Association.

Robertson-Nay, R., & Brown, R. C. (2011). Neurodevelopmental aspects of social anxiety. In C. A. Alfano & D. C. Beidel (Eds.), *Social anxiety in adolescents and young adults: Translating developmental science into practice* (pp. 53–71). Washington, DC: American Psychological Association.

Rubin, K. H., Wojslawowicz, J. C., Rose-Krasnor, L., Booth-LaForce, C., & Burgess, K. B. (2006). The best friendships of shy/withdrawn children: Prevalence, stability, and relationship quality.

Journal of Abnormal Child Psychology, 34, 139–153. doi:10.1007/s10802-005-9017-4

Ruscio, A. M., Brown, T. A., Chiu, W. T., Sareen, J., Stein, M. B., & Kessler, R. C. (2008). Social fears and social phobia in the USA: Results from the national comorbidity survey replication. *Psychological Medicine, 38,* 15–28. doi:10.1017/S0033291707001699

Sachs-Ericsson, N., Verona, E., Joiner, T., & Preacher, K. J. (2006). Parental verbal abuse and the mediating role of self-criticism in adult internalizing disorders. *Journal of Affective Disorders, 93*(1), 71–78. doi:10.1016/j.jad.2006.02.014

Schilder, P. (1938). The social neurosis. *Psychoanalytic Review, 25,* 1–19.

Schneier, F. R., Liebowitz, M. R., Abi-Dargham, A., Zea-Ponce, Y., Lin, S., & Laruelle, M. (2000). Low dopamine D2 receptor binding potential in social phobia. *The Americal Journal of Psychiatry, 157,* 457–459. doi:10.1176/appi.ajp.157.3.457

Schwartz, C. E., Snidman, N., & Kagan, J. (1999). Adolescent social anxiety as an outcome of inhibited temperament in childhood. *Journal of the American Academy of Child and Adolescent Psychiatry, 38,* 1008–1015. doi:10.1097/00004583-199908000-00017

Shipon-Blum, D. E. (n.d.). *What is selective mutism?* Retrieved from http://www.selectivemutismcenter.org/aboutus/WhatisSelectiveMutism

Silverman, L. K. (2007). Perfectionism: The crucible of giftedness. *Gifted Education International, 23,* 233–245. doi:10.1177/026142940702300304

St. Clair, M. C., Pickles, A., Durkin, K., & Conti-Ramsden, G. (2011). A longitudinal study of behavioral, emotional and social difficulties in individuals with a history of specific language impairment (SLI). *Journal of Communication Disorders, 44,* 186–199. doi:10.1016/j.jcomdis.2010.09.004

Starr, L. R., Davila, J., La Greca, A., & Landoll, R. R. (2011). Social anxiety and depression: The teenage and early adult years. In C. A. Alfano & D. C. Beidel (Eds.), *Social anxiety in adolescents and young adults: Translating developmental science into practice* (pp. 75–91). Washington, DC: American Psychological Association.

Stein, M. B., Torgrud, L. J., & Walker, J. R. (2000). Social phobia symptoms, subtypes, and severity: Findings from a community survey. *Archives of General Psychiatry, 57,* 1046–1052. doi:10.1001/archpsyc.57.11.1046

Stein, M. B., & Stein, D. J. (2008). Social anxiety disorder. *The Lancet, 371,* 1115–1125.

Teetsel, R. N., Ginsburg, G. S., &Drake, K. L. (2014). Anxiety-promoting parenting behaviors: A comparison of anxious mothers and fathers. *Child Psychiatry & Human Development, 45,* 133–142. doi:10.1007/s10578-013-0384-8.

U.S. Department of Health and Human Services, Office of Civil Rights. (n.d.). *Section 504.* Retrieved from http://www.hhs.gov/ocr/civilrights/resources/factsheets/504.pdf

Vannest, K. J., Reynolds, C. R., & Kamphaus, R. W. (2008). Interventions for anxiety. In *BASC-2 intervention guide for behavioral and emotional issues* (pp. 275–318). Bloomington, MN: NCS Pearson.

White, S. W., Albano, A., Johnson, C., Kasari, C., Ollendick, T., Klin, A., . . . Scahill, L. (2010). Development of a cognitive-behavioral intervention program to treat social anxiety and social deficits in teens with high-functioning autism. *Clinical Child and Family Psychology Review, 13*(1), 77–90. doi:10.1007/s10567-009-0062-3

White, S. W., Ollendick, T., Scahill, L., Oswald, D., & Albano, A. (2009). Preliminary efficacy of a cognitive-behavioral treatment program for anxious youth with autism spectrum disorders. *Journal of Autism and Developmental Disorders, 39,* 1652–1662. doi:10.1007/s10803-009-0801-9

White, S. W., & Schiry, A. R. (2011). Social anxiety in adolescents on the autism spectrum. In C. A. Alfano & D. C. Beidel (Eds.), *Social anxiety in adolescents and young adults: Translating developmental science into practice* (pp. 183–201). Washington, DC: American Psychological Association.

Wittchen, H. U., Stein, M. B., & Kessler, R. C. (1999). Social fears and social phobia in a community sample of adolescents and young adults: Prevalence, risk factors, and co-morbidity. *Psychological Medicine, 29,* 309–323.

Wood, J. J., McLeod, B. D., Sigman, M., Hwang, W., & Chu, B. C. (2003). Parenting and childhood anxiety: Theory, empirical findings, and future directions. *Journal of Child Psychology and Psychiatry and Allied Disciplines, 44,* 134–151. doi:10.111/1469-7610.00106

Zerr, A. A., Holly, L. E., & Pina, A. A. (2011). Cultural influences on social anxiety in African American, Asian American, Hispanic and Latino, and Native American adolescents and young adults. In C. A. Alfano & D. C. Beidel (Eds.), *Social anxiety in adolescents and young adults: Translating developmental science into practice* (pp. 203–222). Washington, DC: American Psychiatric Association.

About the Author

Critically acclaimed and award-winning nonfiction and fiction author **Christine Fonseca** is dedicated to helping children and adults find their unique voice in the world. In nonfiction, she delves into the world of giftedness, resiliency, and temperament, offering children and adults a no-nonsense, how-to approach to facing the world without fear. She has taught parenting classes for more than a decade, works with educators to understand the social and emotional needs of the gifted, and is a frequent presenter at statewide conferences on topics related to children and education. Christine works as a school psychologist at the elementary, middle, and high school levels. She also coaches children and parents to work through their anxieties.

Christine has written self-help articles for Parents.com, Johnson & Johnson, *Bop/Tiger Beat*, and *Justine Magazine*. She was awarded the 2013 Special Achievement Award from the Surrey International Writer's Conference for her body of work and efforts to give back to the community and was a semifinalist in the Kindle Book Review's Best Indie Book (YA) for her thriller, *Transcend*. Recent titles include *The Girl Guide*, *Quiet Kids*, *Indie and Proud*, and a young adult suspense novel, *Collide*.

Christine lives in the San Diego area with her husband and children. When she isn't crafting new books, she can be found sipping too many skinny vanilla lattes at the local coffee house, or exploring the world with her family. For more information about Christine Fonseca or her books, visit her website http://christinefonseca.com.